Happy Homemade

Sew Chic Kids

20 Designs That Are Fun and Unique—Just Like Your Kid!

Ruriko Yamada

TUTTLE Publishing

Tokyo | Rutland, Vermont | Singapore

How to Make It

All of the patterns are actual size with the exception of some of the ribbons and bias tape.

The patterns are measured according to the size chart below. Sizes are 2, 4, 6 and 8. Please measure the child and choose the correct pattern size accordingly.

Adjust the length of the garment according to the height, leg and torso measurements of the child.

Material lengths and fabric requirements are all written in order of size. Measurements are given in inches with centimeters in brackets. Using the metric measurements will give you a more precise cut.

Pattern placement and seam allowance is detailed in the diagrams; however, they are based on the size 4 pattern. The placement may need to be changed, depending on the size.

Reference sizes

Size	2	4	6	8
Height	39½ (100)	44 (110)	48 (120)	52 (130)
Chest	21¼ (54)	22¾ (58)	24½ (62)	26 (66)
Waist	19¼ (49)	20 (51)	21 (53)	21½ (55)
Hip	22½ (57)	24 (61)	25½ (65)	27½ (70)

Note that elastic allowance for patterns is generous and waist gathering should be adjusted for individual children.

How to measure

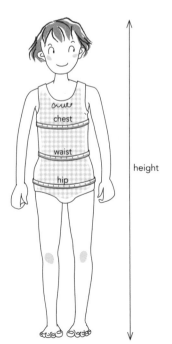

P **Tiered Skirt**

S **Pull-over Parka**

contents

How to Make It...... page 2

a   Dress with Frilled Shoulders...... page 4
b   Dress with Square Neckline...... page 5
c   Ribbon-tied Blouse...... page 6
d   Flared Shorts...... page 7
e   Smock Dress...... page 8
f   Tiered Dress...... page 9
g   Tiered Blouse...... page 10
h   Pin-tucked Blouse...... page 12
i   Roll-up Shorts...... page 13
j   V-neck Dress...... page 14
k   Dress with Flared Sleeves...... page 15
l   Knee-length Shorts...... page 16
m   Shorts with Back Pockets...... page 17
n   Front-buttoned Smock...... page 18
o   Wide-leg Pants...... page 19
p   Tiered Skirt...... page 20
q   Boy's Stand-up Collar Shirt...... page 21
r   Pinafore...... page 22
s   Pull-over Parka...... page 24
t   Boy's Shirt...... page 25

Basic Tools   Needles and Threads...... page 27
Sewing Machine Tips...... page 28
How to Made a Paper Pattern with Seam Allowance...... page 30
Pattern Placement...... page 31
About Fabric...... page 32

Layouts and instructions begin on page 33

a Dress with Frilled Shoulders

For special occasions, the shoulder frill gives a touch of elegance.

Instructions on **page 33**

b Dress with Square Neckline

Basic sleeveless dress with a square yoke and a cute gathered skirt.

Instructions on **page 34**

C Ribbon-tied Blouse

The neckline is fastened with a ribbon.

Instructions on **page 36**

d Flared Shorts

Easy to wear, simple design. The perfect feel-good pants.

Instructions on **page 37**

e Smock Dress

Pin-tucks on the bodice and shirring on the pocket and cuffs.
So cute!

Instructions on page 38

→ blouse

f Tiered Dress

Voluminous, gathered dress. Can be worn back-to-front.
Pictured here with the ribbon at the front.

Instructions on **page 40**

g Tiered Blouse

A two-tiered version of dress **f**.

Instructions on **page 42**

The ribbon is made from the same fabric as the blouse.
Pictured here with the ribbon at the back.

i Roll-up Shorts

Made from linen for that safari feeling.

Instructions on **page 44**

j V-neck Dress

Made from linen, with coordinating lace on neckline and armholes.

Instructions on **page 45**

k Dress with Flared Sleeves

Charming flared sleeves and a ribbon tie. Light and pretty.

Instructions on **page 46**

▌Knee-length Shorts

Elastic waist with a fake fly. So easy to wear.

Instructions on **page 48**

n Shorts with Back Pockets

Perfect casual pants for everyday wear.

Instructions on **page 50**

n Front-buttoned Smock

A bohemian smock. Button-up front and raglan sleeves.

Instructions on **page 52**

Wide-leg Pants

Children can enjoy the grown-up style of long linen pants.

Instructions on **page 54**

p　Tiered Skirt

Use a lightweight fabric with body, for optimal gathering effect.

Instructions on **page 56**

q **Boy's Stand-up Collar Shirt**

Cool-feel shirt with a neat finish on the collar.

Instructions on **page 57**

r Pinafore

Pinafore with frill.

Wear over a singlet or long-sleeved top.

Instructions on **page 58**

Worn by itself as a cool and airy sundress.

S Pull-over Parka

Same shape for boys and girls.

No fastenings means it is easy to sew.

Instructions on **page 60**

✝ **Boy's Shirt**

Cute shirt with a stiffened collar. Wear it neat and look smart.

Instructions on **page 62**

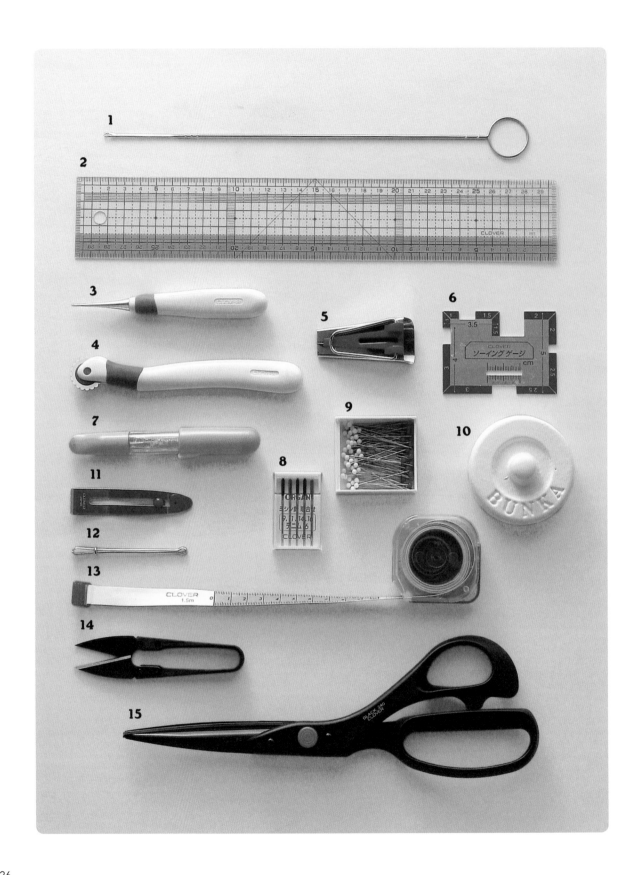

BASIC TOOLS

1 LOOP TURNER
For turning a fabric tube right side out. Useful for making button loops and many types of straps.

2 TRANSPARENT GRAPH RULER
Useful for drawing parallel lines. A must-have item for adding seam allowance.

3 AWL
Useful for punching holes in heavy fabrics and for turning out corners.

4 TRACING WHEEL
Useful for transferring markings from a pattern onto fabric. Can be used with or without paper.

5 TAPE MAKER
Useful for making bias binding. Available in various widths.

6 MINI RULER
Useful for making small measurements. A metal mini-ruler is useful when ironing.

7 DRESSMAKER'S CHALK
For marking fabric. Pictured is a chalk wheel, which contains powdered chalk for making lines of consistent width (unlike regular chalk which becomes thicker as you use it).

8 SEWING-MACHINE NEEDLES
Choose your needle size according to the type of fabric and thread being used. It is important to change the needle when it is damaged or worn to ensure a neat finish.

9 DRESSMAKING PINS
Don't use pins with large heads. Small-headed pins are easy to use.

10 FABRIC WEIGHT
For holding pattern paper in place on your fabric when cutting out.

11 BODKIN (WIDE)
For threading wide elastic through an elastic casing.

12 BODKIN
For threading elastic through an elastic casing. Can also be used for threading other things such as ribbon or wool.

13 TAPE MEASURE
A must-have item. Useful when taking your measurements for sizing and for measuring curves.

14 THREAD SNIPPERS
For snipping threads. Keep with your sewing machine at all times.

15 DRESSMAKING SCISSORS
Preferred size is 9–10 in (23–26 cm). To avoid making the scissors blunt, do not use to cut anything other than fabric.

NEEDLES AND THREADS

An important element in accomplishing a neat finish is the balance of needle, thread and fabric. A good finish cannot be attained just by thread and needle, needle and fabric or thread and fabric: the balance is a combination of all three. A good understanding of different thread types will help you achieve this.

CHARACTERISTICS OF DIFFERENT SEWING-MACHINE THREADS

POLYESTER The most commonly-used thread, as it is cheap and versatile. Suitable for most fabrics.
NYLON More flexible than polyester, used with knit fabrics.
SILK Very strong and rather expensive, it is not used much these days. Polyester thread is best for sewing silk fabric.
COTTON Like silk thread, cotton thread is strong, but not frequently used as it is more expensive than polyester.

MATCHING SEWING-MACHINE NEEDLES TO THE THREAD

SIZE 9 Very thin—used with #90 thread.
SIZE 11 Medium—used on most fabrics with #60 or #50 thread.
SIZE 14 Thick—used on thick fabrics with #50 or #60 thread. If you wish to highlight stitching, use #30 thread.
SIZE 16 Very thick—used on thick, heavy fabrics. It stitches well on canvas. Can be used with #60, #50 and #30 thread.

DIFFERENT THREAD SIZES

A larger number indicates a thinner thread.
#90 Used to sew very thin fabrics, such as lawn cloth and voile.
#60 #50 The most commonly-used sizes, suitable for use on most fabrics.
#30 Used for decorative stitching.

Needle	Thread	Fabric
Size 9	#90	Lawn cloth, voile, silk, satin, etc.
Size 11	#60 #50	Broadcloth, gingham, soft denim, chino, flannel, etc.
Size 14	#60 #50 #30	Thick denim, thick sewing tape, etc.
Size 16	#60 #50 #30	Canvas, thick sewing tape, etc.

SEWING MACHINE TIPS

Here are a few simple tips to improve your machine-sewing techniques.

TO START SEWING

1 Thread the needle from front to back. Once threaded, hold the thread then lower and raise the needle completely so it picks up the bobbin thread from below. Pull the two threads out together to the other side.

2 Align the fabric edge with the marker on the bobbin plate according to the seam allowance (in this case 3/8 in/1 cm). When in position, lower the foot.

3 It is possible for fabric to get caught under the needle hole, so make sure you hold both threads back. This will enable a neat start.

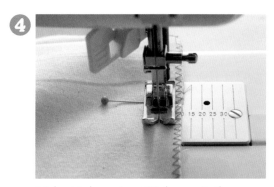

4 It is best to have pins at 90 degrees to the sewing line. This allows smooth stitching and ensures that the sewing-machine needle is not damaged.

5 Use both hands when sewing, as pictured above, to prevent fabric from slipping or moving and to ensure edges are aligned.

SEWING CLOSE TO AN EDGE

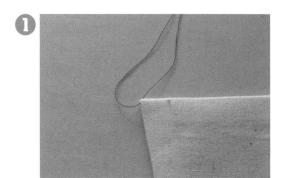

When sewing a narrow section, sometimes the fabric gets drawn into the hole under the foot. Sew a thread on the corner as shown in the picture.

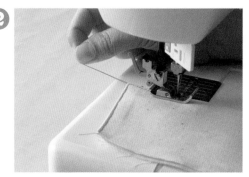

To prevent the fabric from being pulled into the hole under the foot, exercise caution and hold the thread when sewing.

SEWING CORNERS

When sewing on a square pocket, for example, sew towards the corner, but stop before you get to the edge. Sew the last 2–3 stitches manually, using the wheel to raise and lower the needle.

Use the wheel to lower the needle to its lowest position, then raise the foot.

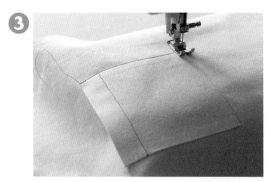

With the needle down and the foot raised, turn the fabric around 90 degrees. Lower the foot and sew to the next corner.

If you need to do a double stitch, you can use the first line as a guide. Depending on the width of the double stitching, you could also use the lines on the foot as a guide.

HOW TO MAKE A PAPER PATTERN WITH SEAM ALLOWANCE

When tracing the patterns in this book, we recommend you add the seam allowances onto the pattern as you draw. It takes extra time but reduces the chance of mistakes and makes it easier to sew later on. Be sure to trace the entire pattern and include all notches, stitching lines, pocket placement lines, etc.

PATTERN AS SHOWN IN BOOK

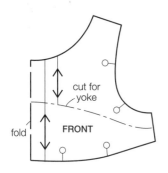

ACTUAL PATTERNS AFTER CUTTING

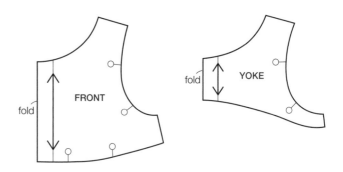

HOW TO TRACE PATTERN ONTO PAPER

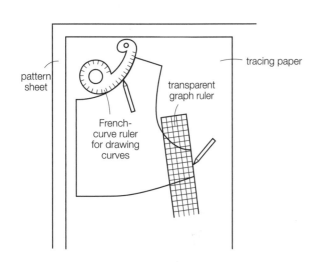

HOW TO DRAW SEAM ALLOWANCE

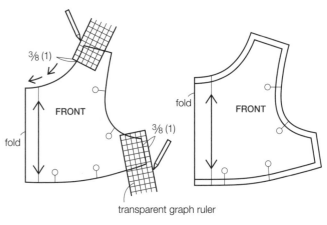

WIDTH OF ALLOWANCE

Unless otherwise specified, seam allowance is $3/8$ in (1 cm).
If you are using a zip or fastener, make a $5/8$ in (1.5 cm) allowance.
If there are triple folds, follow the instructions.
The direction in which darts are folded determines how they should be cut. To ensure accuracy, fold the pattern in the required direction before cutting the darts.

PATTERN PLACEMENT

Key techniques for fabric alignment, pattern placement and cutting.

HOW TO FOLD AND ALIGN FABRICS

Measure the fabric accurately. Fold in half lengthwise and check that the pattern fits onto the fabric. Place pattern edge on the fold of the fabric and ensure that the fabric thread is parallel to the direction of the grain line.

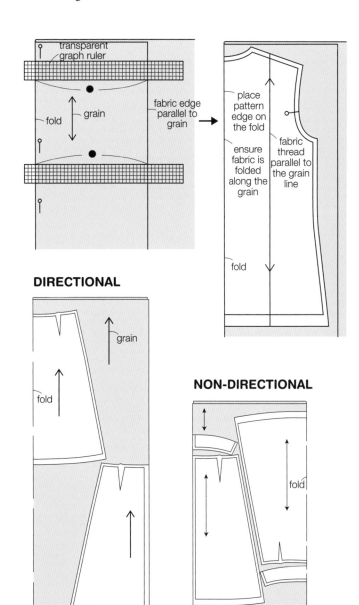

CUTTING PATTERNED FABRIC

Ensure that you check the direction of the fabric and the pattern before cutting. When cutting plain fabric or fabric with a non-directional print (a print that has no wrong or right way up), place the paper pattern onto the fabric as shown in the diagram on the far right.

If the fabric has a pile going up (e.g. velvet), or a directional print, place the pattern pieces in the same direction, as shown in the diagram. For checked fabrics, ensure that the lines meet and are symmetrical

PATTERN DIRECTION INDICATORS

Follow the arrow on the paper pattern when placing onto fabric. Ensure the fabric runs in the same direction as the arrow. There are exceptions, such as when cutting on the bias, or if your fabric is not wide enough, you can place the pattern lengthways. If necessary, you can cut pieces such as the yoke or pocket in a different direction, or in another fabric altogether.

PATTERN PLACEMENT

Place the pattern, with the added seam allowance, onto the fabric. The best method to hold the pattern in place on the fabric is to use weights, however you can also use pins.

ABOUT FABRIC

Understanding fabric types will help you select the right fabric when buying.

WIDTH

Different fabric types come in a variety of widths. Cotton is usually about 44 in (110–112 cm) wide but it is also available at 35½ in (90 cm) wide. Wool is often 56 in (142 cm). Linen or interior fabrics can be 71 in (180 cm) wide. Fabrics for non-commercial sewing are usually 44 in (110–112 cm). Sometimes this is not wide enough for your pattern, so always check the instructions for the width of the fabric required before you buy.

TYPES OF FABRIC

Fabrics are made from natural and artificial fibers. Cotton, hemp, silk and wool are made from natural fibers, and polyester and nylon are made from artificial fibers. It is good to understand the different characteristics of fibers and materials to enable you to make an informed choice when selecting the best fabric for your pattern.

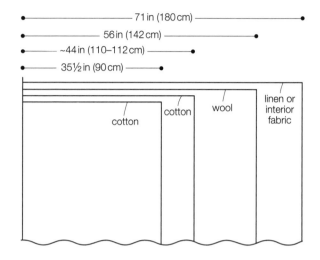

HOW TO STRAIGHTEN THE FABRIC

In times past, all fabrics had to be pre-washed and then straightened. Today, only linen and cotton fabrics need to be straightened. If you are unable to cut straight along the side (weft) thread when cutting vertically from selvage to selvage, that means your fabric is not straight. Wash the fabric and, while it is wet, pull it into shape. In most cases this will fix the problem and your fabric will be straightened.

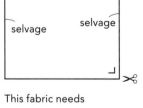

This fabric needs straightening.

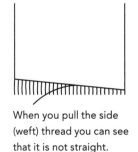

When you pull the side (weft) thread you can see that it is not straight.

Cut off the bottom threads along the side (weft) thread.

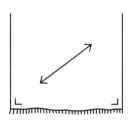

While fabric is wet, pull the corners into right angles.

a Dress with Frilled Shoulders page 4

pattern pieces

a back; a front; a back yoke & back yoke facing;
  a front yoke & front yoke facing; a frill

materials

44 in (110 cm) print polyester: 48 in (1.2 m) [size 2];
  52 in (1.3 m) [size 4]; 55½ in (1.4 m) [size 6];
  59 in (1.5 m) [size 8]
½ in (1.2 cm) buttons x 2

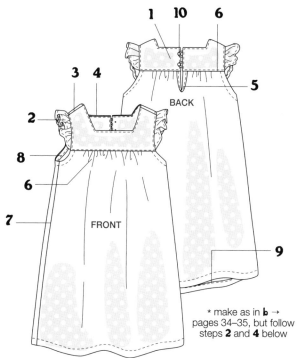

* make as in **b** →
pages 34–35, but follow
steps **2** and **4** below

2 make sleeve frill

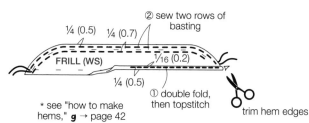

¼ (0.5) ¼ (0.7)
② sew two rows of basting
FRILL (WS)
1/16 (0.2)
¼ (0.5)
① double fold, then topstitch
trim hem edges

* see "how to make hems," **g** → page 42

↓

FRILL (RS)   press gathers

gather frill to fit between notches on armhole

* make two the same

4 sew yoke pieces with sleeve frills

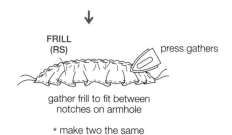

④ turn RS out

3/8 (1)

① fold front and back yoke facing hems and press

FRONT YOKE FACING (WS)

FRONT YOKE (RS)

BACK YOKE FACING (WS)

② sew yoke and yoke facing together, enclosing frill

¼ (0.5)

BACK YOKE (RS)

FRILL (WS)

button loops

¼ (0.5) 3/8 (1)

3/8 (1)

BACK YOKE (RS)

③ trim seam allowance to ¼ (0.5)

[LAYOUT]

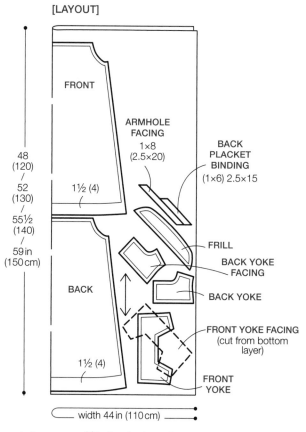

48 (120) / 52 (130) / 55½ (140) / 59 in (150 cm)

FRONT

1½ (4)

BACK

1½ (4)

ARMHOLE FACING 1×8 (2.5×20)

BACK PLACKET BINDING (1×6) 2.5×15

FRILL

BACK YOKE FACING

BACK YOKE

FRONT YOKE FACING (cut from bottom layer)

FRONT YOKE

width 44 in (110 cm)

* all seams are 3/8 in (1 cm) unless otherwise specified

* measurements are shown in order of size

33

b Dress with Square Neckline page 5

pattern pieces

b back; b front; b back yoke & back yoke facing;
   b front yoke & front yoke facing

materials

42 in (106 cm) cotton gingham: 49 in (1.25 m) [size 2];
   52 in (1.3 m) [size 4]; 55½ in (1.4 m) [size 6];
   59 in (1.5 m) [size 8]
⅜ in (1.1 cm) buttons x 2

10 sew buttons to back yoke

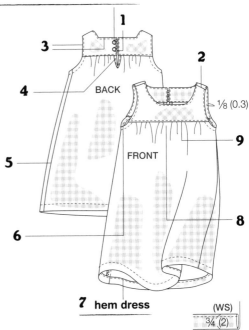

7 hem dress

[LAYOUT]

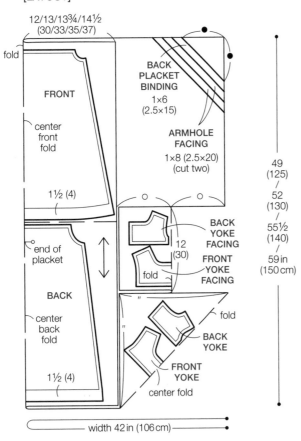

12/13/13¾/14½
(30/33/35/37)

fold

FRONT

center
front
fold

1½ (4)

end of
placket

BACK

center
back
fold

1½ (4)

BACK
PLACKET
BINDING
1×6
(2.5×15)

ARMHOLE
FACING
1×8 (2.5×20)
(cut two)

BACK
YOKE
FACING

12
(30)

FRONT
YOKE
FACING

fold

BACK
YOKE

FRONT
YOKE

fold

center fold

49
(125)
/
52
(130)
/
55½
(140)
/
59 in
(150 cm)

— width 42 in (106 cm) —

* all seams are ⅜ in (1 cm) unless otherwise specified

* measurements are shown in order of size

1 make loop

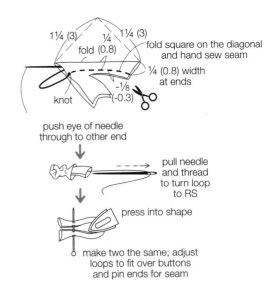

push eye of needle
through to other end

pull needle
and thread
to turn loop
to RS

press into shape

make two the same; adjust
loops to fit over buttons
and pin ends for seam

2 sew shoulder seams

3 sew yoke and yoke lining together

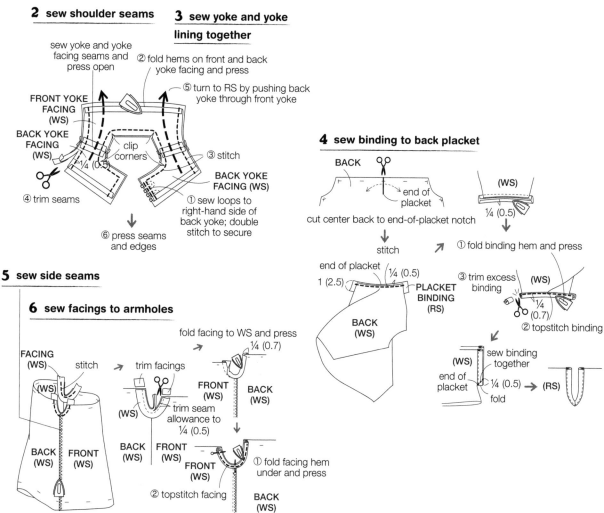

sew yoke and yoke facing seams and press open

② fold hems on front and back yoke facing and press

⑤ turn to RS by pushing back yoke through front yoke

FRONT YOKE FACING (WS)

BACK YOKE FACING (WS)

clip corners

¼ (0.5)

④ trim seams

③ stitch

BACK YOKE FACING (WS)

① sew loops to right-hand side of back yoke; double stitch to secure

⑥ press seams and edges

4 sew binding to back placket

BACK

end of placket

cut center back to end-of-placket notch

stitch

(WS)

¼ (0.5)

① fold binding hem and press

③ trim excess binding

(WS)

¼ (0.7)

② topstitch binding

end of placket

1 (2.5)

¼ (0.5)

PLACKET BINDING (RS)

BACK (WS)

(WS)

sew binding together

end of placket

¼ (0.5)

fold

(RS)

5 sew side seams

6 sew facings to armholes

FACING (WS)

stitch

(WS)

BACK (WS)

FRONT (WS)

trim facings

fold facing to WS and press

¼ (0.7)

FRONT (WS)

BACK (WS)

(WS)

trim seam allowance to ¼ (0.5)

BACK (WS)

FRONT (WS)

FRONT (WS)

① fold facing hem under and press

② topstitch facing

BACK (WS)

8 how to gather

sew two rows of basting using a long stitch (about ¼/0.5)

¼ (0.5)

¼ (0.7)

gather between notches

FRONT (RS)

gather evenly until top edge matches lower edge of yoke

to gather, pull the two bobbin threads

press gathers

* repeat with back yoke

9 sew yoke to dress

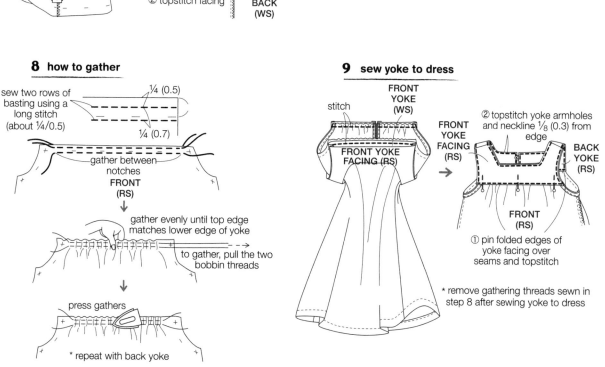

stitch

FRONT YOKE (WS)

FRONT YOKE FACING (RS)

FRONT YOKE FACING (RS)

② topstitch yoke armholes and neckline ⅛ (0.3) from edge

BACK YOKE (RS)

FRONT (RS)

① pin folded edges of yoke facing over seams and topstitch

* remove gathering threads sewn in step 8 after sewing yoke to dress

35

C Ribbon-tied Blouse

page 6

pattern pieces

c back; c front; c back yoke; c front yoke; c sleeve

materials

44 in (110 cm) floral-print cotton: 33½ in (0.85 m) [size 2];
35½ in (0.9 m) [size 4]; 37½ in (0.95 m) [size 6];
41¼ in (1.05 m) [size 8]

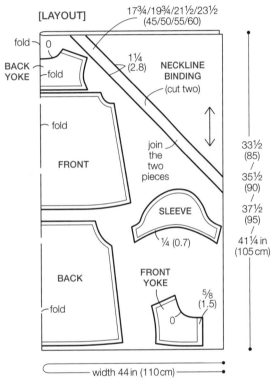

[LAYOUT]

17¾/19¾/21½/23½
(45/50/55/60)

fold — 0

BACK YOKE — fold

1¼ (2.8)

NECKLINE BINDING (cut two)

fold

FRONT

join the two pieces

33½ (85)
/
35½ (90)
/
37½ (95)
/
41¼ in (105 cm)

SLEEVE

¼ (0.7)

BACK — fold

FRONT YOKE

⅝ (1.5)

0

— width 44 in (110 cm) —

* all seams are ⅜ in (1 cm) unless otherwise specified
* measurements are shown in order of size

* make as in **k** → pages 46–47, but follow steps **6** and **7** below

7 hem blouse

¼ (0.5)

6 make sleeves

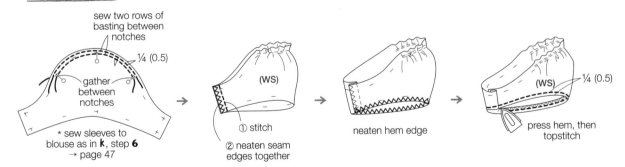

sew two rows of basting between notches

¼ (0.5)

gather between notches

* sew sleeves to blouse as in **k**, step **6** → page 47

* match all sleeve notches to armhole notches

(WS)

① stitch

② neaten seam edges together

neaten hem edge

(WS)

¼ (0.5)

press hem, then topstitch

pattern pieces

d back; d front

materials

46½ in (118 cm) lightweight denim:

    17¾ in (0.45 m) [size 2]; 27½ in (0.7 m) [size 4];

    31½ in (0.8 m) [size 6]; 35½ in (0.9 m) [size 8]

¾ in (2 cm) elastic: 25½ in (65 cm)

[LAYOUT]

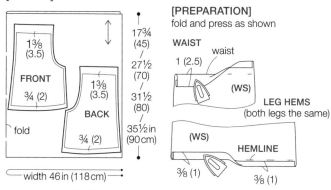

[PREPARATION]
fold and press as shown

WAIST

LEG HEMS
(both legs the same)

HEMLINE

* all seams are ⅜ in (1 cm) unless otherwise specified

* measurements are shown in order of size

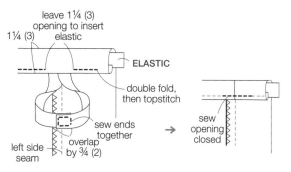

5 topstitch pant hems

1 sew side seams

LEFT LEG BACK (RS)

LEFT LEG FRONT (WS)

press side seams towards back (repeat for right leg)

neaten seam edges together

2 sew inside-leg seams

press inside-leg seams towards back (repeat for right leg)

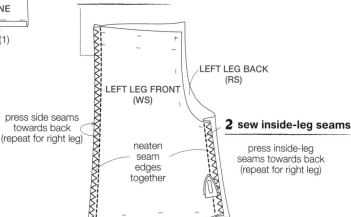

3 sew crotch seam

insert one leg into the other

side seam

RIGHT LEG BACK (WS)

reinforce with two rows of stitching

left and right leg backs together

left and right leg fronts together

inside-leg seam

RIGHT LEG FRONT (RS)

LEFT LEG FRONT (WS)

LEFT LEG FRONT (WS)

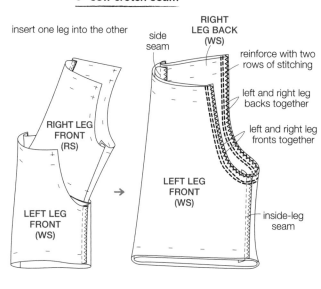

4 make elastic casing and insert elastic

leave 1¼ (3) opening to insert elastic

1¼ (3)

ELASTIC

double fold, then topstitch

sew ends together

left side seam

overlap by ¾ (2)

sew opening closed

e Smock Dress

page 8

pattern pieces

e back; e front; e sleeve; e pocket

materials

41¼ in (105 cm) cotton double gauze:
    53 in (1.35 m) [size 2]; 57 in (1.45 m) [size 4]
    61 in (55 m) [size 6]; 65 in (1.65 m) [size 8]
print cotton for binding: 16 in x 16 in (40 cm x 40 cm)
¼ in (0.7 cm) elastic: 35½ in (90 cm)

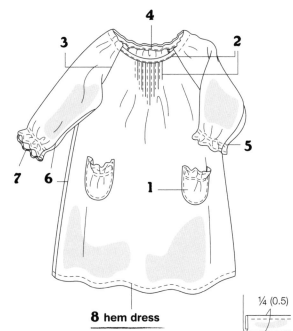

8 hem dress

¼ (0.5)

1 make pockets

① double fold to ¼ (0.5),
then topstitch

(WS)

neaten
edges

② sew a row of
basting 1/16 (0.2) from
the seam line

(WS)

use a card template
to shape pocket

gather basting and
press pocket hem

[LAYOUT]

COTTON DOUBLE GAUZE

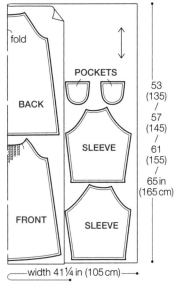

fold

POCKETS

BACK

SLEEVE

FRONT

SLEEVE

53 (135)
57 (145)
61 (155)
65 in (165 cm)

width 41¼ in (105 cm)

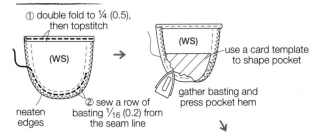

POCKET (WS)

¾ (2)

⅛ (0.4)

stretch elastic
across pocket and
sew with two rows
of stitching

⅜ (1)

(WS)

elastic
3¾ (9.5)
long

elastic should not
overlap seam
allowance

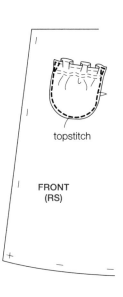

topstitch

FRONT (RS)

PRINT COTTON

19¾ (50)

1¼ (3)

NECKLINE FACING

1¼ (3)

20 (8)

width 16 in (40 cm)

FRONT NECKLINE BINDING

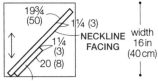

width 16 in (40 cm)

* all seams are ⅜ in (1 cm) unless otherwise specified

* measurements are shown in order of size

38

2 sew pintucks and front neckline binding

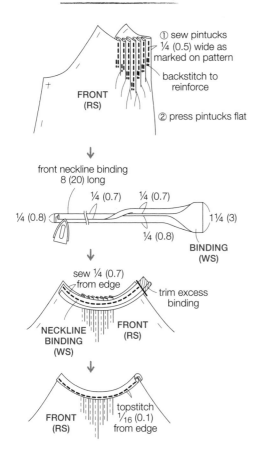

① sew pintucks ¼ (0.5) wide as marked on pattern

backstitch to reinforce

FRONT (RS)

② press pintucks flat

front neckline binding 8 (20) long

¼ (0.7) ¼ (0.7)

¼ (0.8)

¼ (0.8)

1¼ (3)

BINDING (WS)

sew ¼ (0.7) from edge

trim excess binding

NECKLINE BINDING (WS)

FRONT (RS)

FRONT (RS)

topstitch ¹⁄₁₆ (0.1) from edge

3 sew sleeves to dress

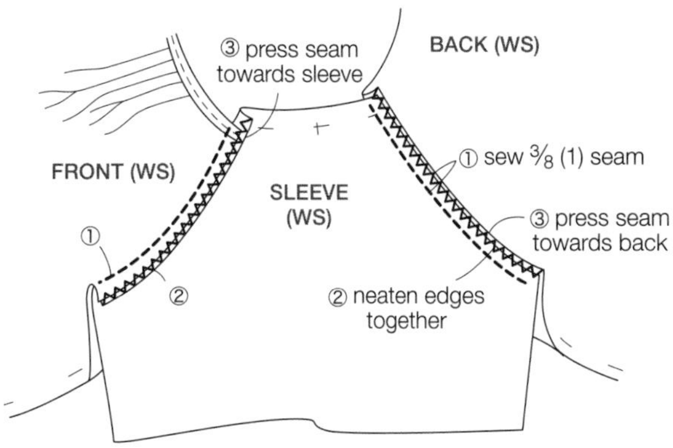

③ press seam towards sleeve

BACK (WS)

FRONT (WS)

SLEEVE (WS)

① sew ⅜ (1) seam

③ press seam towards back

② neaten edges together

①

②

4 sew neckline facing and insert elastic

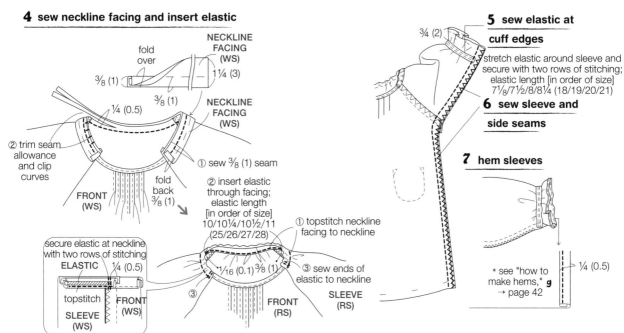

fold over

NECKLINE FACING (WS)

⅜ (1)

1¼ (3)

⅜ (1)

¼ (0.5)

NECKLINE FACING (WS)

② trim seam allowance and clip curves

FRONT (WS)

fold back ⅜ (1)

① sew ⅜ (1) seam

② insert elastic through facing; elastic length [in order of size] 10/10¼/10½/11 (25/26/27/28)

① topstitch neckline facing to neckline

secure elastic at neckline with two rows of stitching

ELASTIC ¼ (0.5)

topstitch

FRONT (WS)

SLEEVE (WS)

③

¹⁄₁₆ (0.1) ⅜ (1)

FRONT (RS)

③ sew ends of elastic to neckline

SLEEVE (RS)

5 sew elastic at cuff edges

¾ (2)

stretch elastic around sleeve and secure with two rows of stitching; elastic length [in order of size] 7⅛/7½/8/8¼ (18/19/20/21)

6 sew sleeve and side seams

7 hem sleeves

* see "how to make hems," **g**
→ page 42

¼ (0.5)

f Tiered Dress

page 9

2
7
1
FRONT
4
3
6
BACK
5

pattern pieces

f top tier back; f top tier front; f middle tier;
f bottom tier

materials

42 in (106 cm) print cotton: 61 in (1.55 m) [size 2];
65 in (1.65 m) [size 4]; 71 in (1.8 m) [size 6];
2 yd 3 in (1.9 m) [size 8]

1¼ in (3 cm) ribbon: 49 in (125 cm)

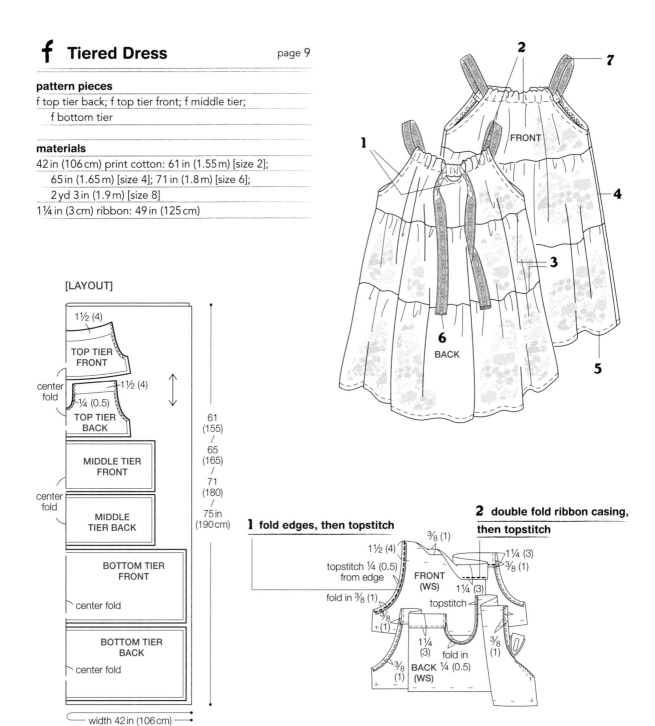

[LAYOUT]

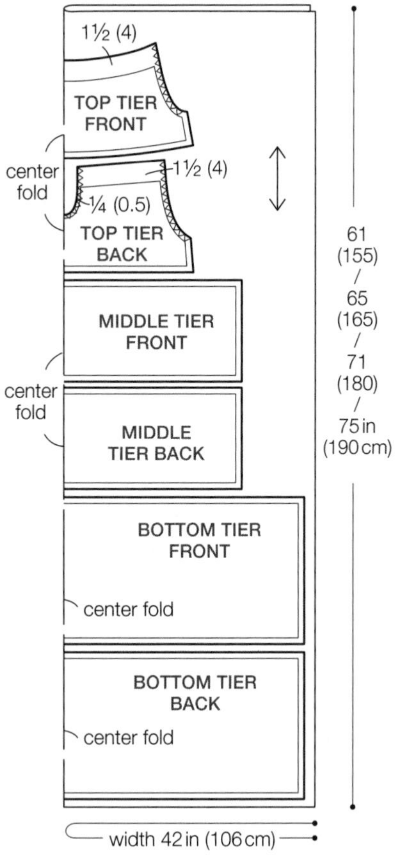
1½ (4)
TOP TIER FRONT
center fold
1½ (4)
¼ (0.5)
TOP TIER BACK
MIDDLE TIER FRONT
center fold
MIDDLE TIER BACK
BOTTOM TIER FRONT
center fold
BOTTOM TIER BACK
center fold
61 (155) / 65 (165) / 71 (180) / 75 in (190 cm)
width 42 in (106 cm)

1 fold edges, then topstitch

2 double fold ribbon casing, then topstitch

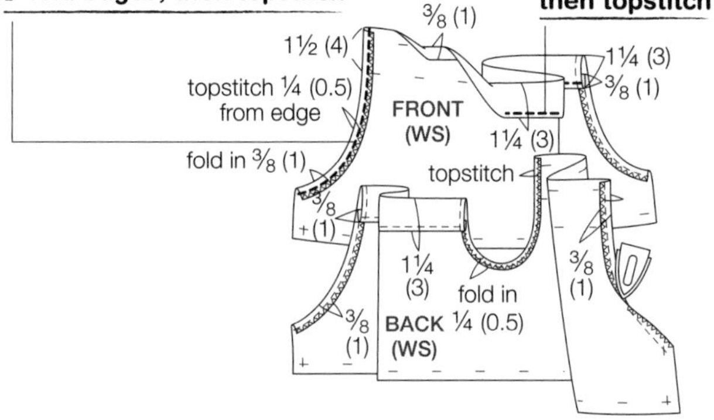
⅜ (1)
1½ (4)
topstitch ¼ (0.5) from edge
fold in ⅜ (1)
FRONT (WS)
1¼ (3)
topstitch
1¼ (3)
⅜ (1)
⅜ (1)
1¼ (3)
fold in ¼ (0.5)
⅜ (1)
BACK (WS)
⅜ (1)

* all seams are ⅜ in (1 cm) unless otherwise specified
* measurements are shown in order of size
* ~~~ neaten edges using an overlocker or zig-zag stitch before sewing

3 sew tiers together

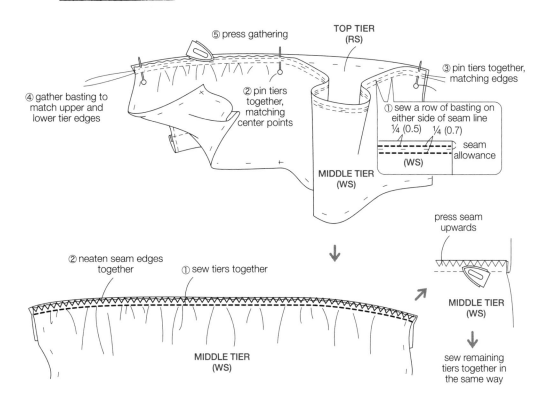

⑤ press gathering

TOP TIER
(RS)

④ gather basting to match upper and lower tier edges

② pin tiers together, matching center points

③ pin tiers together, matching edges

① sew a row of basting on either side of seam line
¼ (0.5)   ¼ (0.7)

seam allowance

(WS)

MIDDLE TIER
(WS)

press seam upwards

MIDDLE TIER
(WS)

sew remaining tiers together in the same way

② neaten seam edges together

① sew tiers together

MIDDLE TIER
(WS)

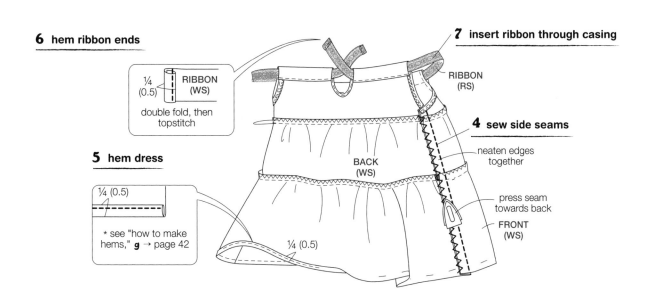

6 hem ribbon ends

¼ (0.5)   RIBBON
(WS)

double fold, then topstitch

7 insert ribbon through casing

RIBBON
(RS)

5 hem dress

¼ (0.5)

* see "how to make hems," **g** → page 42

BACK
(WS)

¼ (0.5)

4 sew side seams

neaten edges together

press seam towards back

FRONT
(WS)

g Tiered Blouse

page 10

pattern pieces

g top tier back; g top tier front; g bottom tier

materials

40 in (102 cm) herringbone cotton:

48 in (1.2 m) [size 2]; 49 in (1.25 m) [size 4];

52 in (1.3 m) [size 6]; 55½ in (1.4 m) [size 8]

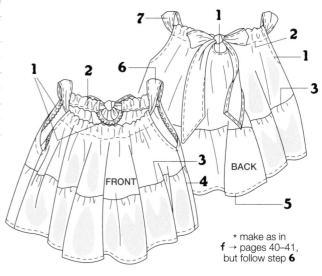

* make as in
f → pages 40–41,
but follow step **6**

[LAYOUT]

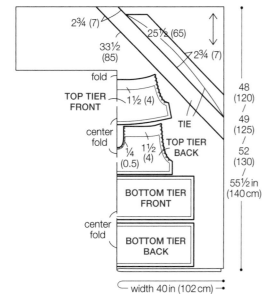

width 40 in (102 cm) [unfolded]

2¾ (7)

25½ (65)

33½ (85)

2¾ (7)

fold

TOP TIER FRONT

1½ (4)

TIE

center fold

¼ (0.5)

1½ (4)

TOP TIER BACK

BOTTOM TIER FRONT

center fold

BOTTOM TIER BACK

48 (120)

49 (125)

52 (130)

55½ in (140 cm)

width 40 in (102 cm)

* all seams are ⅜ in (1 cm) unless otherwise specified

* measurements are shown in order of size

* ∿∿ neaten edges using an overlocker or zig-zag stitch before sewing

6 make tie

tie is 56 (142) before hemming

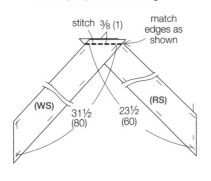

stitch ⅜ (1)

match edges as shown

(WS)

(RS)

31½ (80)

23½ (60)

HOW TO MAKE HEMS

☆ when working with lightweight fabric, make the hem-folds thin; it enhances the lightness of the fabric

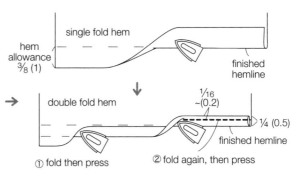

single fold hem

hem allowance ⅜ (1)

finished hemline

double fold hem

¹⁄₁₆ ~(0.2)

¼ (0.5)

finished hemline

① fold then press   ② fold again, then press

to make tie, hem all four edges in this way

h Pin-tucked Blouse

pattern pieces

h back; h front; h sleeve

materials

44 in (110 cm) print polyester: 35½ in (0.9 m) [size 2];
   37½ in (0.95 m) [size 4]; 39½ in (1 m) [size 6];
   57 in (1.45 m) [size 8]
¼ in (0.7 cm) elastic: 31½ in (80 cm)

[LAYOUT]

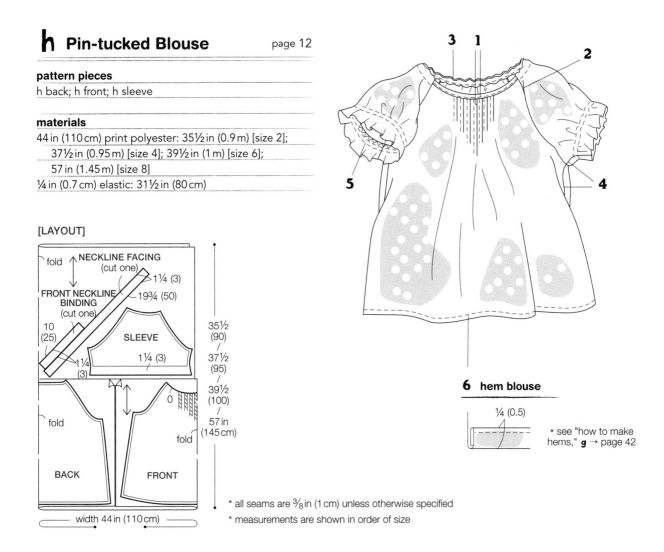

NECKLINE FACING (cut one)
1¼ (3)
19¾ (50)
FRONT NECKLINE BINDING (cut one)
fold
10 (25)
SLEEVE
1¼ (3)
1¼ (3)
35½ (90)
37½ (95)
39½ (100)
57 in (145 cm)
fold
fold
0
BACK
FRONT
width 44 in (110 cm)

* all seams are ⅜ in (1 cm) unless otherwise specified
* measurements are shown in order of size

6 hem blouse

¼ (0.5)

* see "how to make hems," **g** → page 42

4 sew side and sleeve seams

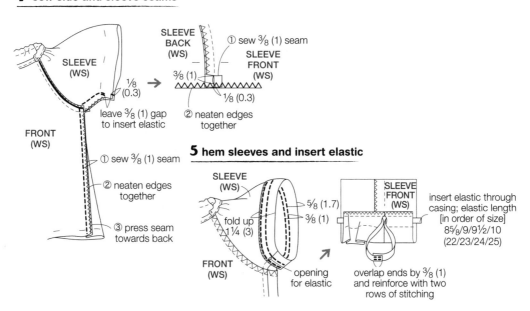

SLEEVE (WS)
⅛ (0.3)
leave ⅜ (1) gap to insert elastic

SLEEVE BACK (WS)
① sew ⅜ (1) seam
SLEEVE FRONT (WS)
⅜ (1)
⅛ (0.3)
② neaten edges together

FRONT (WS)
① sew ⅜ (1) seam
② neaten edges together
③ press seam towards back

5 hem sleeves and insert elastic

SLEEVE (WS)
⅝ (1.7)
⅜ (1)
fold up 1¼ (3)
FRONT (WS)
opening for elastic

SLEEVE FRONT (WS)
insert elastic through casing; elastic length [in order of size]
8⅝/9/9½/10 (22/23/24/25)
overlap ends by ⅜ (1) and reinforce with two rows of stitching

43

¡ Roll-up Shorts

page 13

pattern pieces

i back; i front; i side pocket; i back pocket;
   i fly facing & fly shield; i waistband; i tab

materials

21 in (53 cm) hemp linen: 63 in (1.6 m) [size 2];
   67 in (1.7 m) [size 4]; 71 in (1.8 m) [size 6];
   2 yd 11 in (2.1 m) [size 8]
¾ in (2 cm) elastic: 25½ in (65 cm)
½ in (1.3 cm) buttons x 4

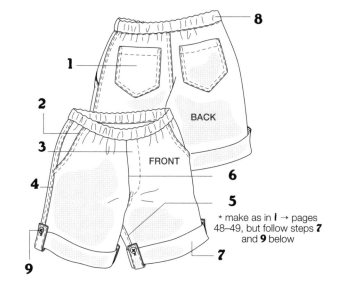

* make as in **l** → pages 48–49, but follow steps **7** and **9** below

[LAYOUT]
SIZE 8

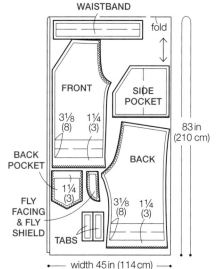

width 45 in (114 cm)

SIZES 2, 4 & 6

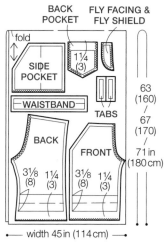

63 (160)
67 (170)
71 in (180 cm)

width 45 in (114 cm)

* all seams are ⅜ in (1 cm) unless otherwise specified
* measurements are shown in order of size
* ∿∿∿ neaten edges using an overlocker or zig-zag stitch before sewing

7 make tabs and cuffs

[PREPARATION]
fold and press as shown

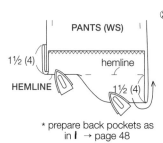

PANTS (WS)

1½ (4)

hemline

HEMLINE   1½ (4)

* prepare back pockets as in **l** → page 48

press tab as shown

① fold in half lengthwise, then topstitch

⅜ (1)
¼ (0.5)
topstitch 1⁄16 (0.2) from edge
② make buttonhole

(WS)

* make four the same

¾ (2)

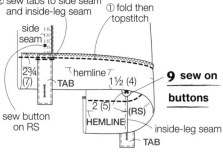

② sew tabs to side seam and inside-leg seam

① fold then topstitch

side seam

2¾ (7)   TAB

hemline

1½ (4)

sew button on RS

9 sew on buttons

2 (5)   (RS)
HEMLINE
inside-leg seam
TAB

j V-neck Dress

page 14

pattern pieces

j back; j front; j back yoke; j front yoke

materials

59 in (150 cm) linen: 31½ in (0.8 m) [size 2];
 33½ in (0.85 m) [size 4]; 35½ in (0.9 m) [size 6];
 37½ in (0.95 m) [size 8]
¼ in (0.7 cm) lace braid: 42 in (106 cm)

[LAYOUT]

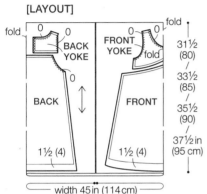

* all seams are ⅜ in (1 cm) unless otherwise specified
* measurements are shown in order of size
* ∿∿ neaten edges using an overlocker or zig-zag stitch before sewing

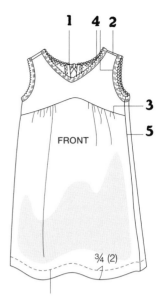

6 double fold hem,

then topstitch

1 make back placket

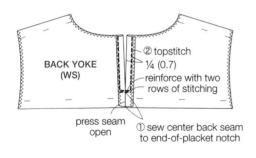

② topstitch ¼ (0.7)
reinforce with two rows of stitching
press seam open
① sew center back seam to end-of-placket notch

2 sew shoulder seams

3 sew front and back yokes to dress

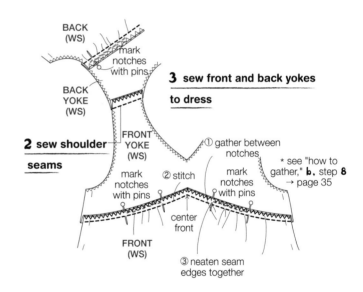

mark notches with pins
① gather between notches
* see "how to gather," **b**, step **8** → page 35
② stitch
center front
③ neaten seam edges together

4 sew on lace braid

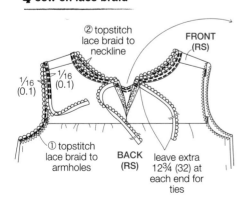

② topstitch lace braid to neckline
1/16 (0.1)   1/16 (0.1)
① topstitch lace braid to armholes
BACK (RS)
leave extra 1¾ (32) at each end for ties

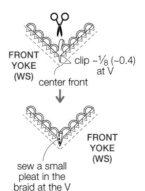

clip ~⅛ (~0.4) at V
FRONT YOKE (WS)
center front
FRONT YOKE (WS)
sew a small pleat in the braid at the V

5 sew side seams

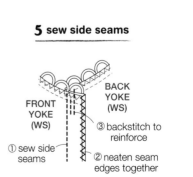

FRONT YOKE (WS)
BACK YOKE (WS)
① sew side seams
② neaten seam edges together
③ backstitch to reinforce

k Dress with Flared Sleeves page 15

pattern pieces

k back; k front; k back yoke; k front yoke; k sleeve

materials

40 in (120 cm) London-stripe cotton:
   49 in (1.25 m) [size 2]; 52 in (1.3 m) [size 4];
   55½ in (1.4 m) [size 6]; 73 in (1.85 m) [size 8]

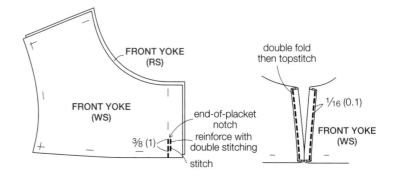

7 topstitch dress hem

(WS)

¾ (2)

[LAYOUT]

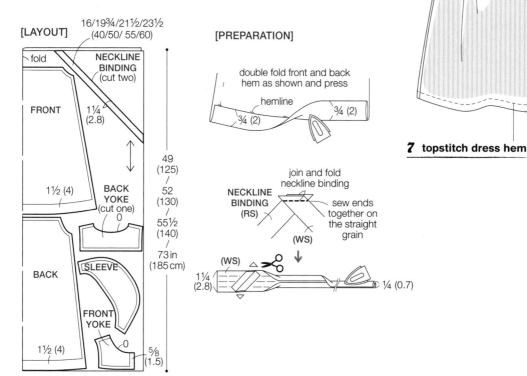

16/19¾/21½/23½
(40/50/ 55/60)

fold

NECKLINE
BINDING
(cut two)

FRONT

1¼ (2.8)

1½ (4)

BACK
YOKE
(cut one)
0

49 (125) /
52 (130) /
55½ (140) /
73 in (185 cm)

BACK

SLEEVE

FRONT
YOKE

1½ (4)

0

5⁄8 (1.5)

width 40 in (102 cm)

* all seams are 3⁄8 in (1 cm) unless otherwise specified

* measurements are shown in order of size

* unless otherwise specified, neaten all seam edges together using an overlocker or zigzag stitch

[PREPARATION]

double fold front and back hem as shown and press

hemline

¾ (2)

¾ (2)

join and fold neckline binding

NECKLINE
BINDING
(RS)

sew ends together on the straight grain

(WS)

(WS)

1¼ (2.8)

¼ (0.7)

1 make front yoke opening

FRONT YOKE
(RS)

FRONT YOKE
(WS)

end-of-placket notch
reinforce with double stitching

3⁄8 (1)

stitch

double fold then topstitch

1⁄16 (0.1)

FRONT YOKE
(WS)

2 sew shoulder seams

BACK YOKE (WS)

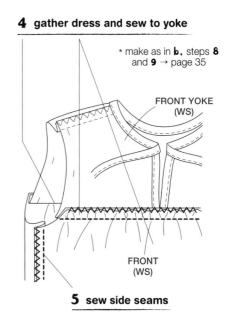

1/16 (0.1)

1/4 (0.7)

3 sew on neckline binding

① sew on binding

1/16 (0.1)

② fold binding over raw edge and topstitch

FRONT YOKE (WS)

1/4 (0.7)

10 (25)

double fold end by 1/4 (0.5)

topstitch

4 gather dress and sew to yoke

* make as in **b**, steps **8** and **9** → page 35

FRONT YOKE (WS)

FRONT (WS)

5 sew side seams

6 sew sleeves

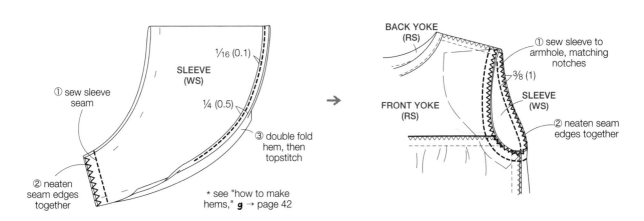

1/16 (0.1)

SLEEVE (WS)

① sew sleeve seam

1/4 (0.5)

③ double fold hem, then topstitch

② neaten seam edges together

* see "how to make hems," **g** → page 42

BACK YOKE (RS)

① sew sleeve to armhole, matching notches

3/8 (1)

FRONT YOKE (RS)

SLEEVE (WS)

② neaten seam edges together

▎Knee-length Shorts

pattern pieces

1 back; 1 front; 1 side pocket; 1 back pocket;
  1 fly facing & fly shield; 1 waistband

materials

45 in (114 cm) cotton chino cloth: 31½ in (0.8 m) [size 2];
  33½ in (0.85 m) [size 4]; 35½ in (0.9 m) [size 6];
  37½ in (0.95 m) [size 8]
¾ in (2 cm) elastic: 25½ in (65 cm)

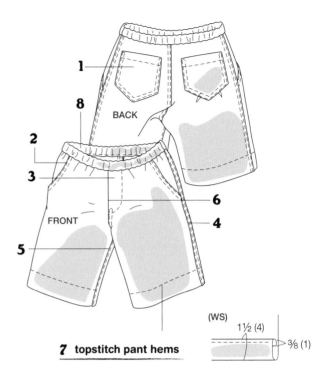

[LAYOUT]

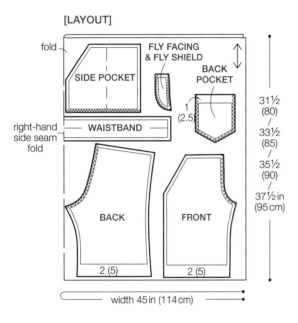

fold

FLY FACING
& FLY SHIELD

SIDE POCKET

BACK
POCKET

1
(2.5)

WAISTBAND

right-hand
side seam
fold

BACK

FRONT

2 (5)

2 (5)

31½
(80)

33½
(85)

35½
(90)

37½ in
(95 cm)

◀ width 45 in (114 cm) ▶

* all seams are ⅜ in (1 cm) unless otherwise specified

* measurements are shown in order of size

* ∿∿ neaten edges using an overlocker or zig-zag
stitch before sewing

▎sew back pockets

double fold to ⅝ (1.5),
then topstitch

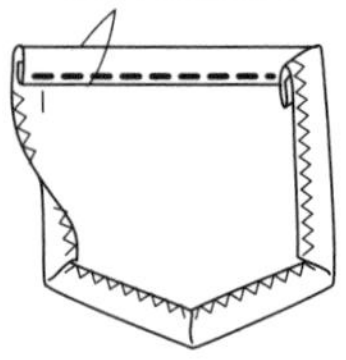

* sew to pants back as in
  o, step **1** → page 55

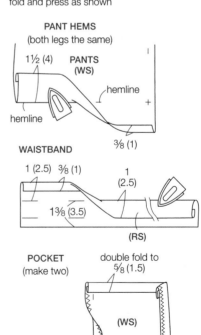

BACK

FRONT

7 topstitch pant hems

(WS)

1½ (4)

⅜ (1)

[PREPARATION]
fold and press as shown

PANT HEMS
(both legs the same)

1½ (4)   PANTS
(WS)

hemline

hemline

⅜ (1)

WAISTBAND

1 (2.5)   ⅜ (1)

1
(2.5)

1⅜ (3.5)

(RS)

POCKET
(make two)

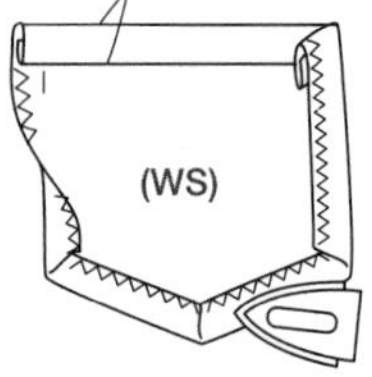

double fold to
⅝ (1.5)

(WS)

2 sew side pockets

pocket opening edge

POCKET TOP (WS)

pocket underlay

RIGHT LEG FRONT (RS)

① fold in half

POCKET TOP (WS)

RIGHT LEG FRONT (WS)

② sew pocket bottom edges together

③ baste pocket to leg

1/16 (0.1)
1/4 (0.7)

RIGHT LEG FRONT (RS)

POCKET TOP (WS)

1/16 (0.1)

topstitch to end of seam

RIGHT LEG FRONT (RS)

FLY SHIELD (RS)

3 sew fly facing and shield

FLY SHIELD (WS)

FLY FACING (WS)

sew to center front

RIGHT LEG FRONT (RS)

LEFT LEG FRONT (RS)

FLY SHIELD (WS)

POCKET TOP (WS)

POCKET TOP (WS)

(RS)

press fly shield to center front and topstitch

RIGHT LEG FRONT (RS)

LEFT LEG FRONT (RS)

press fly facing to WS

4 sew side seams

③ reinforce with two rows of topstitching on leg back

① sew side seam and press to back

1/16 (0.1)
1/4 (0.5)

LEFT LEG BACK (WS)

LEFT LEG FRONT (WS)

② neaten seam edges together

6 sew crotch seam

reinforce crotch seams with two rows of stitching

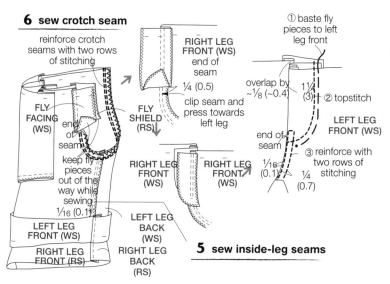

FLY FACING (WS)

end of seam

keep fly pieces out of the way while sewing

1/16 (0.1)

LEFT LEG FRONT (WS)

RIGHT LEG FRONT (RS)

LEFT LEG BACK (WS)

RIGHT LEG BACK (RS)

RIGHT LEG FRONT (WS)

end of seam

1/4 (0.5)

clip seam and press towards left leg

FLY SHIELD (RS)

RIGHT LEG FRONT (WS)

RIGHT LEG FRONT (WS)

① baste fly pieces to left leg front

overlap by ~1/8 (~0.4)

1 1/4 (3)

② topstitch

LEFT LEG FRONT (WS)

end of seam

③ reinforce with two rows of stitching

1/16 (0.1)
1/4 (0.7)

5 sew inside-leg seams

8 sew on waistband and insert elastic

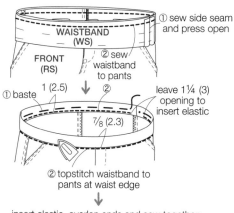

WAISTBAND (WS)

① sew side seam and press open

FRONT (RS)

② sew waistband to pants

① baste

1 (2.5)

②

7/8 (2.3)

leave 1 1/4 (3) opening to insert elastic

② topstitch waistband to pants at waist edge

insert elastic, overlap ends and sew together; sew opening closed

* insert elastic as in ⋔, step **5** → page 51

m Shorts with Back Pockets page 17

pattern pieces

m back; m front; m pocket

materials

44 in (10 cm) cotton: 25½ in (65 cm) [size 2];
27½ in (0.7 m) [size 4]; 29½ in (0.75 m) [size 6];
37½ in (0.95 m) [size 8]

¾ in (2 cm) elastic: 25½ in (65 cm)

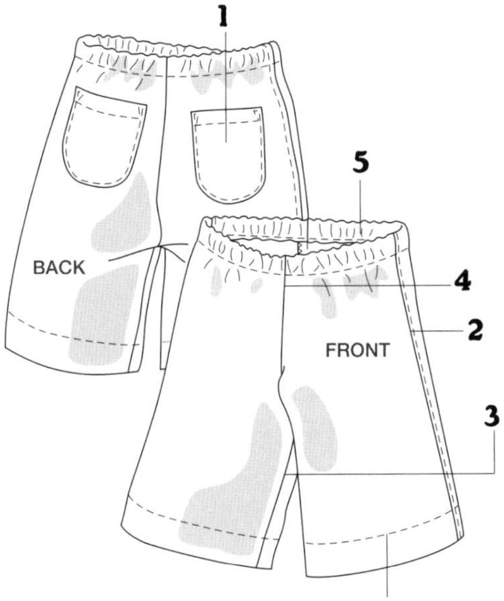

1
5
BACK
4
2
FRONT
3

[LAYOUT]

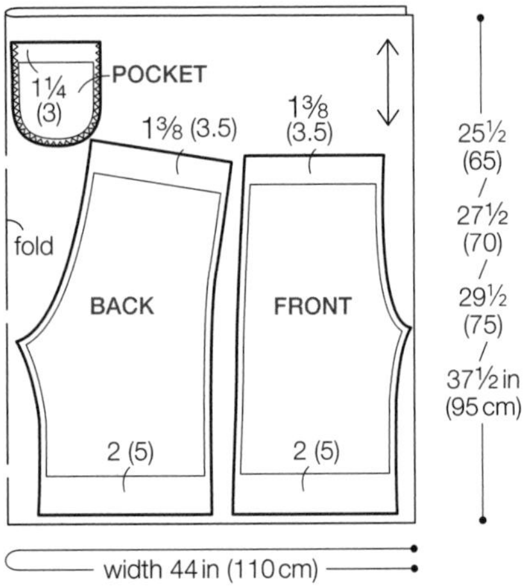

1¼ (3)
POCKET
1⅜ (3.5)
1⅜ (3.5)
fold
BACK
FRONT
2 (5)
2 (5)
25½ (65) / 27½ (70) / 29½ (75) / 37½ in (95 cm)
width 44 in (110 cm)

* all seams are ⅜ in (1 cm) unless otherwise specified

* measurements are shown in order of size

* ~~~ neaten edges using an overlocker or zig-zag stitch before sewing

[PREPARATION]

fold and press as shown

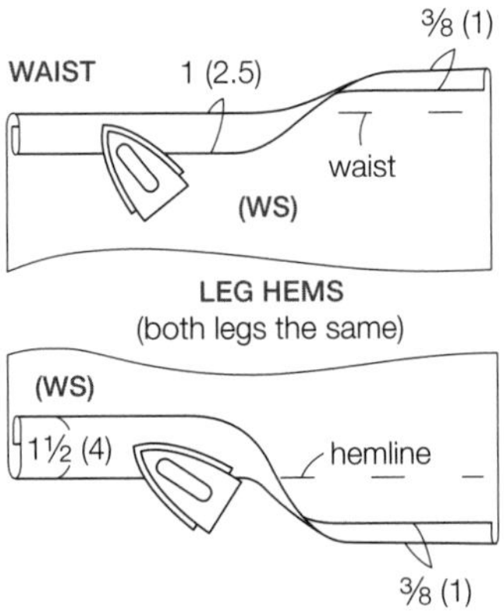

⅜ (1)
WAIST
1 (2.5)
waist
(WS)
LEG HEMS
(both legs the same)
(WS)
1½ (4)
hemline
⅜ (1)

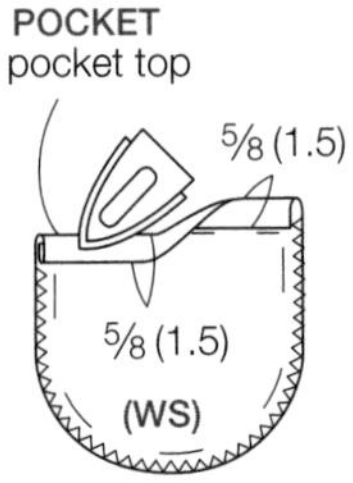

POCKET
pocket top
⅝ (1.5)
⅝ (1.5)
(WS)

6 topstitch pant hems

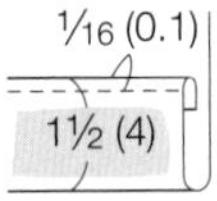

1⁄16 (0.1)
1½ (4)

1 sew pockets

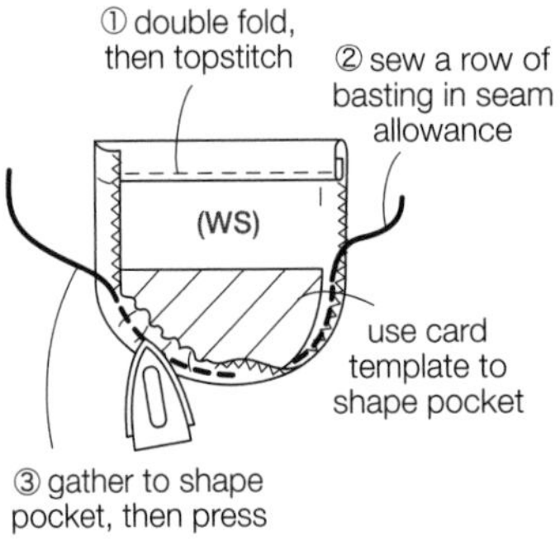

① double fold, then topstitch
② sew a row of basting in seam allowance
(WS)
use card template to shape pocket
③ gather to shape pocket, then press

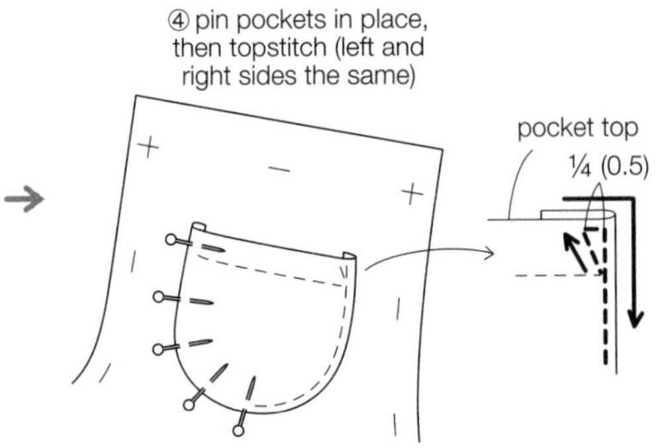

④ pin pockets in place, then topstitch (left and right sides the same)
pocket top
¼ (0.5)

2 sew side seams

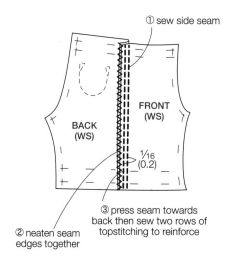

① sew side seam

BACK
(WS)

FRONT
(WS)

$\frac{1}{16}$ (0.2)

③ press seam towards back then sew two rows of topstitching to reinforce

② neaten seam edges together

4 sew crotch seam

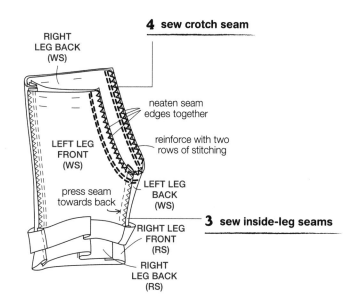

RIGHT LEG BACK (WS)

neaten seam edges together

reinforce with two rows of stitching

LEFT LEG FRONT (WS)

LEFT LEG BACK (WS)

press seam towards back

RIGHT LEG FRONT (RS)

RIGHT LEG BACK (RS)

3 sew inside-leg seams

5 make elastic casing and insert elastic

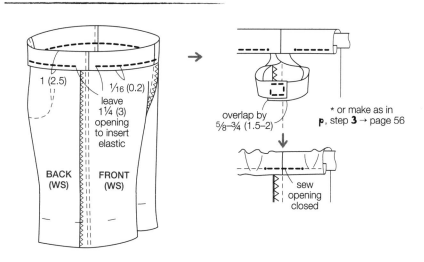

1 (2.5)

$\frac{1}{16}$ (0.2)

leave 1¼ (3) opening to insert elastic

BACK (WS)

FRONT (WS)

overlap by ⅝–¾ (1.5–2)

sew opening closed

* or make as in **p**, step **3** → page 56

⋔ Front-buttoned Smock page 18

pattern pieces

n back; n front; n sleeve; n sleeve frill

materials

48 in (120 cm) cotton linen: 35½ in (0.9 m) [size 2];
　　37½ in (0.95 m) [size 4]; 41½ in (1.05 m) [size 6];
　　52 in (1.3 m) [size 8]
⅝ in (1.5 cm) lace: 2⅜ in (6 cm)
⅜ in (1.1 cm) buttons x 3

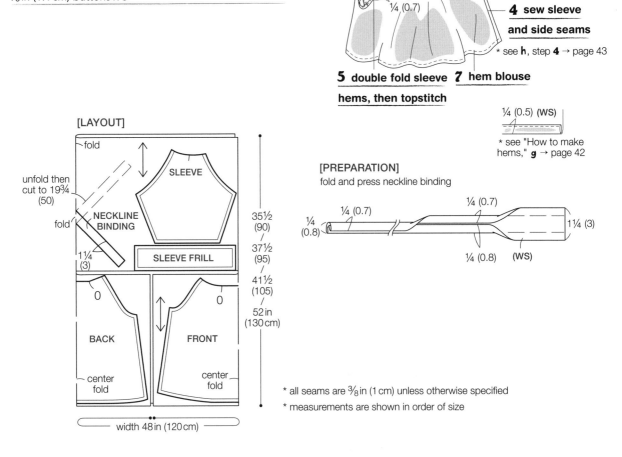

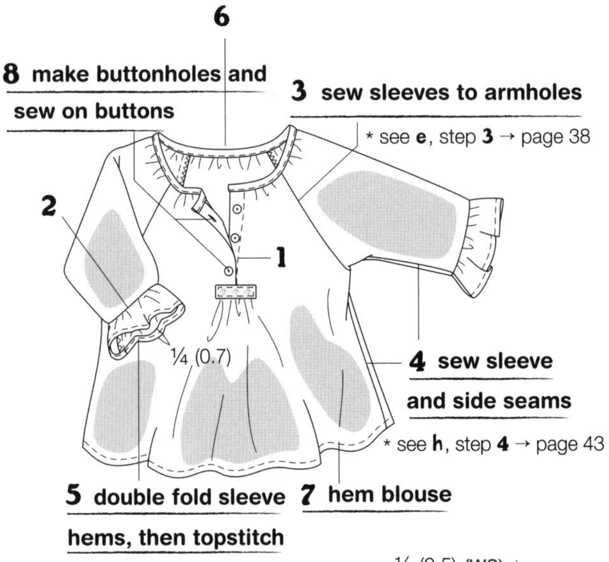

6

8 make buttonholes and
sew on buttons

2

3 sew sleeves to armholes
* see **e**, step **3** → page 38

1

4 sew sleeve
and side seams
* see **h**, step **4** → page 43

¼ (0.7)

5 double fold sleeve
hems, then topstitch

7 hem blouse

¼ (0.5) (WS)

* see "How to make
hems," **g** → page 42

[PREPARATION]
fold and press neckline binding

¼ (0.7)　　¼ (0.7)
¼ (0.8)　　　　　　　　1¼ (3)
¼ (0.8)　(WS)

[LAYOUT]

fold

unfold then
cut to 19¾
(50)

fold

NECKLINE
BINDING

SLEEVE

SLEEVE FRILL

1¼
(3)

0　　　　　　0

BACK　　　FRONT

center
fold　　　center
　　　　　fold

35½
(90)
/
37½
(95)
/
41½
(105)
/
52 in
(130 cm)

width 48 in (120 cm)

* all seams are ⅜ in (1 cm) unless otherwise specified
* measurements are shown in order of size

---

1 make front placket

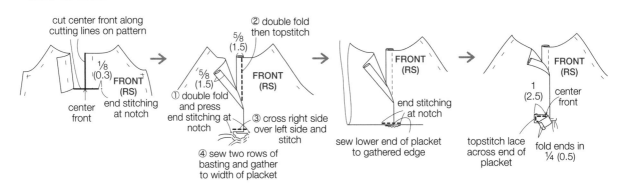

cut center front along
cutting lines on pattern

⅛
(0.3)　FRONT
(RS)

center
front　end stitching
at notch

② double fold
then topstitch

⅝
(1.5)

⅝
(1.5)

① double fold
and press
end stitching at
notch

③ cross right side
over left side and
stitch

④ sew two rows of
basting and gather
to width of placket

FRONT
(RS)

FRONT
(RS)

end stitching
at notch

sew lower end of placket
to gathered edge

FRONT
(RS)

1
(2.5)

center
front

topstitch lace
across end of
placket

fold ends in
¼ (0.5)

2 sew frill to sleeve

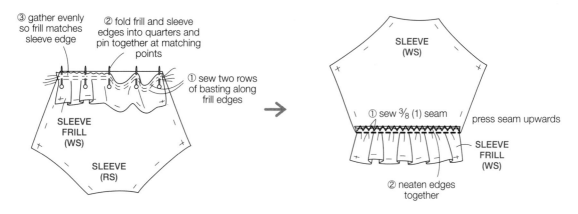

③ gather evenly so frill matches sleeve edge

② fold frill and sleeve edges into quarters and pin together at matching points

① sew two rows of basting along frill edges

SLEEVE FRILL (WS)

SLEEVE (RS)

SLEEVE (WS)

① sew ⅜ (1) seam

press seam upwards

SLEEVE FRILL (WS)

② neaten edges together

6 sew binding to neckline

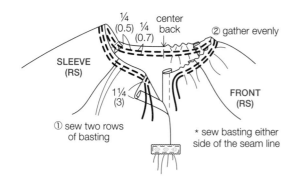

¼ (0.5) ¼ (0.7) center back

② gather evenly

SLEEVE (RS)

1¼ (3)

① sew two rows of basting

FRONT (RS)

* sew basting either side of the seam line

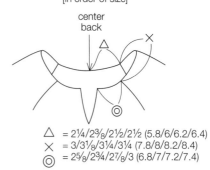

GATHERED NECKLINE LENGTHS
[in order of size]

center back

△ = 2¼/2⅜/2½/2½ (5.8/6/6.2/6.4)
✕ = 3/3⅛/3¼/3¼ (7.8/8/8.2/8.4)
◎ = 2⅝/2¾/2⅞/3 (6.8/7/7.2/7.4)

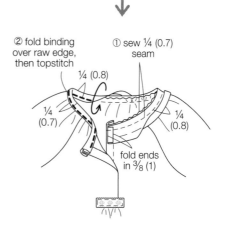

② fold binding over raw edge, then topstitch

① sew ¼ (0.7) seam

¼ (0.8)

¼ (0.7)

¼ (0.8)

fold ends in ⅜ (1)

O Wide-leg Pants

page 19

pattern pieces

o back; o front; o back pocket

materials

21 in (53 cm) hemp linen: 67 in (1.70 m) [size 2]; 71 in (1.8 m) [size 4]; 3 yd 3 in (2.8 m) [size 6]; 3 yd 26 in (3.4 m) [size 8]

¾ in (2 cm) elastic: 25½ in (65 cm)

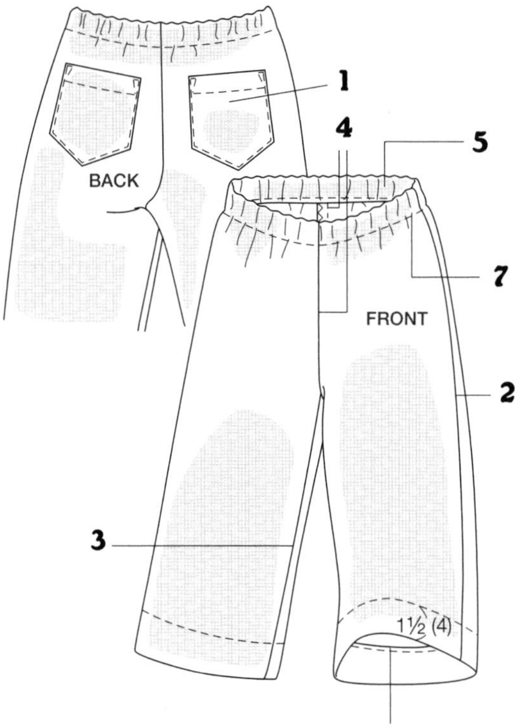
1
4
5
BACK
7
FRONT
2
3
1½ (4)

6 topstitch pant hems

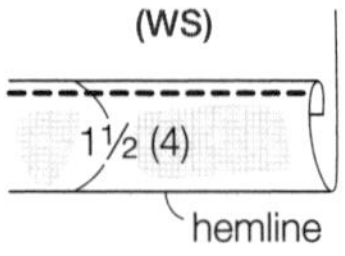
(WS)
1½ (4)
hemline

[LAYOUT]

SIZES 6 AND 8

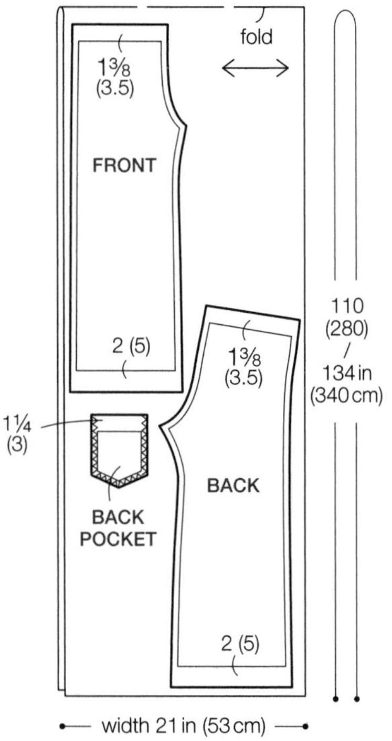
fold
1⅜
(3.5)
FRONT
2 (5)
1⅜
(3.5)
110
(280)
/
134 in
(340 cm)
1¼
(3)
BACK
BACK
POCKET
2 (5)
width 21 in (53 cm)

SIZES 2 AND 4

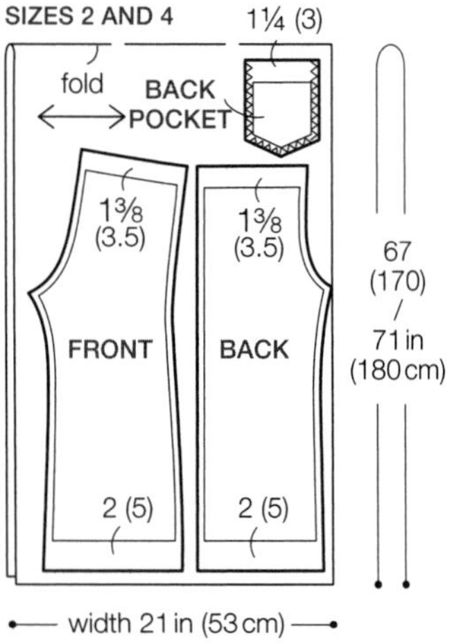
1¼ (3)
fold
BACK
POCKET
1⅜
(3.5)
1⅜
(3.5)
FRONT
BACK
67
(170)
/
71 in
(180 cm)
2 (5)
2 (5)
width 21 in (53 cm)

[PREPARATION]

fold and press hems

BACK POCKET
(make two)

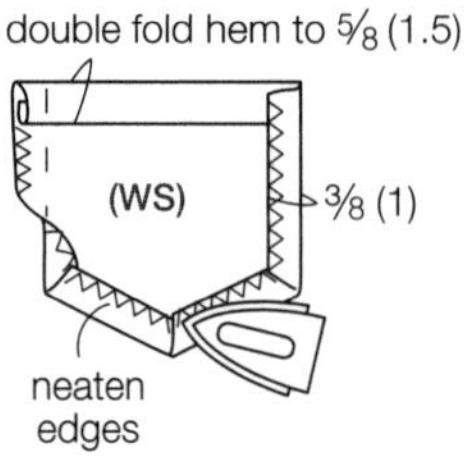
double fold hem to ⅝ (1.5)
(WS)
⅜ (1)
neaten
edges

PANT HEMS
(both legs the same)

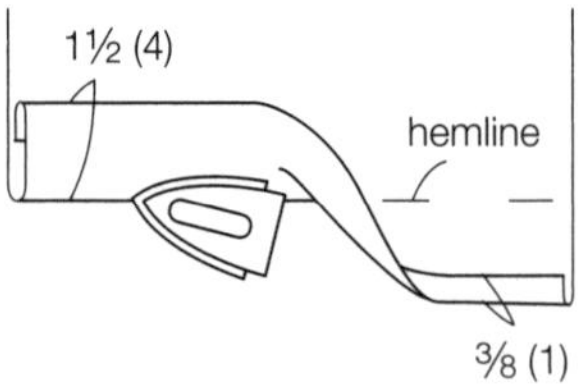
1½ (4)
hemline
⅜ (1)

* all seams are ⅜ in (1 cm) unless otherwise specified

* measurements are shown in order of size

* 〰 neaten edges using an overlocker or zig-zag stitch before sewing

1 **make back pockets**

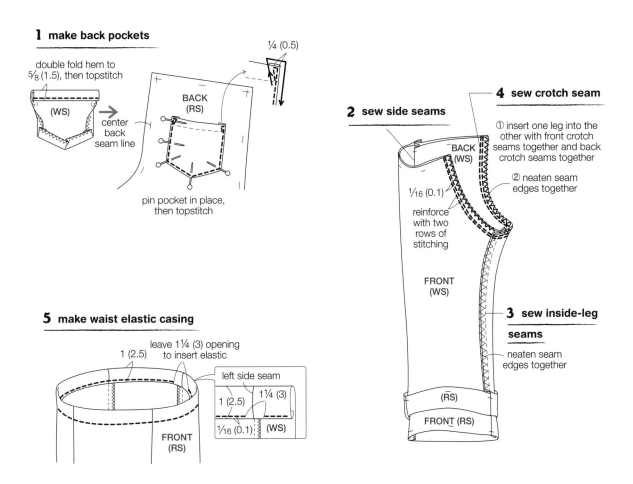

double fold hem to ⅝ (1.5), then topstitch

(WS)

→ center back seam line

¼ (0.5)

BACK (RS)

pin pocket in place, then topstitch

2 **sew side seams**

4 **sew crotch seam**

① insert one leg into the other with front crotch seams together and back crotch seams together

② neaten seam edges together

BACK (WS)

1/16 (0.1)

reinforce with two rows of stitching

FRONT (WS)

3 **sew inside-leg seams**

neaten seam edges together

(RS)

FRONT (RS)

5 **make waist elastic casing**

leave 1¼ (3) opening to insert elastic

1 (2.5)

left side seam

1 (2.5)   1¼ (3)

1/16 (0.1)   (WS)

FRONT (RS)

7 **insert waist elastic**

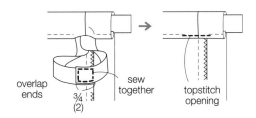

overlap ends

¾ (2)

sew together

topstitch opening

p Tiered Skirt

page 20

pattern pieces

p top tier; p middle tier; p bottom tier

materials

44 in (110 cm) Liberty-print cotton: 31½ in (0.8 m) [size 2];

33½ in (0.85 m) [size 4]; 44 in (1.1 m) [size 6];

45½ in (1.15 m) [size 8]

¾ in (2 cm) elastic: 25½ in (65 cm)

[LAYOUT]

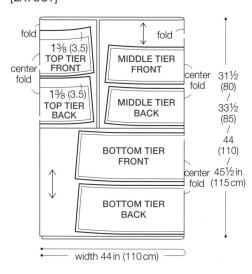

* all seams are ⅜ in (1 cm) unless otherwise specified

* measurements are shown in order of size

2 sew side seams

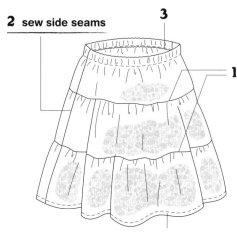

4 double fold hem, then topstitch

¼ (0.5) (WS)

* see "how to make hems," **g** → page 42

1 sew tiers together

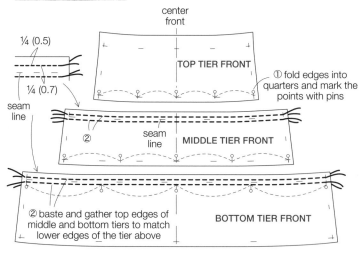

center front

¼ (0.5)

¼ (0.7)

seam line

TOP TIER FRONT

① fold edges into quarters and mark the points with pins

seam line

② MIDDLE TIER FRONT

② baste and gather top edges of middle and bottom tiers to match lower edges of the tier above

BOTTOM TIER FRONT

↓

① sew tiers together along seam line between rows of basting

② neaten seam edges together

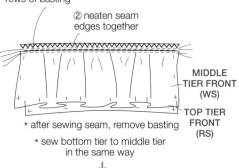

MIDDLE TIER FRONT (WS)

TOP TIER FRONT (RS)

* after sewing seam, remove basting

* sew bottom tier to middle tier in the same way

↓

join back tiers in the same way

3 make elastic casing,

then insert elastic

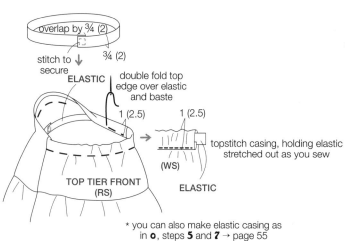

overlap by ¾ (2)

stitch to secure

ELASTIC

¾ (2)

double fold top edge over elastic and baste

1 (2.5)   1 (2.5)

topstitch casing, holding elastic stretched out as you sew

TOP TIER FRONT (RS)

(WS)

ELASTIC

* you can also make elastic casing as in **o**, steps **5** and **7** → page 55

q Boy's Stand-up Collar Shirt page 21

pattern pieces

q back; q front; q sleeve; q yoke & yoke facing; q collar

materials

44 in (110 cm) striped cotton: 35½ in (0.9 m) [size 2];
 37½ in (0.95 m) [size 4]; 39½ in (1 m) [size 6];
 41¼ in (1.05 m) [size 8]

[LAYOUT]

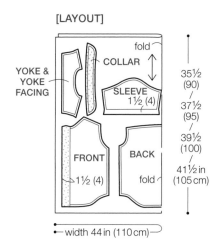

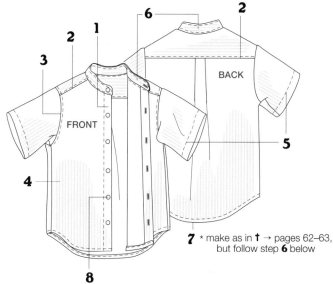

7 * make as in **†** → pages 62–63, but follow step **6** below

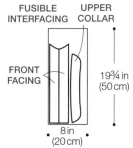

* all seams are ⅜ in (1 cm) unless otherwise specified

* measurements are shown in order of size

* ▨▨▨ apply interfacing to these pieces

* apply interfacing to upper collar only

6 make collar

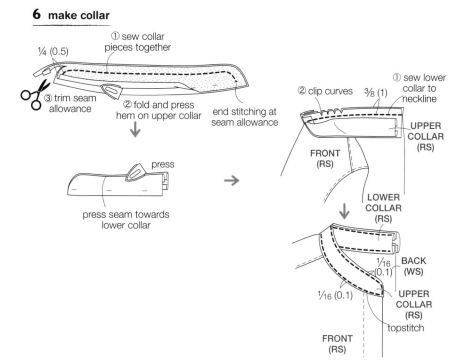

┏ Pinafore

page 22

pattern pieces

r back; r front; r back yoke & back yoke facing;
r front yoke & front yoke facing; r frill

materials

44 in (110 cm) lightweight corduroy:
55½ in (1.4 m) [size 2]; 57 in (1.45 m) [size 4];
59 in (1.5 m) [size 6]; 61 in (1.55 m) [size 8]
⅝ in (1.5 cm) buttons x 2

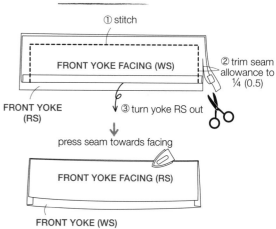

7 topstitch dress hem

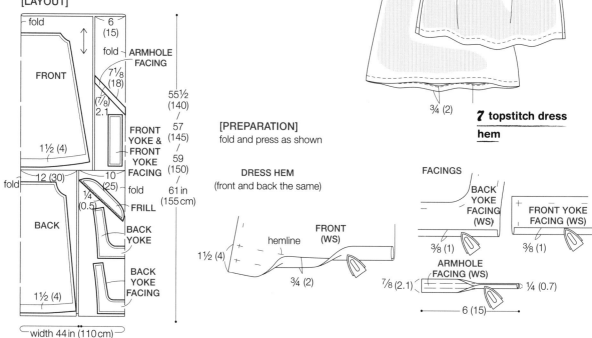

[LAYOUT]

width 44 in (110 cm)

[PREPARATION]
fold and press as shown

DRESS HEM
(front and back the same)

FACINGS

* all seams are ⅜ in (1 cm) unless otherwise specified

* measurements are shown in order of size

* ∿∿ neaten edges using an overlocker or zig-zag stitch before sewing

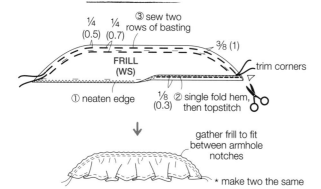

1 sew sleeve frills

③ sew two rows of basting
¼ (0.5) ¼ (0.7) ⅜ (1)
FRILL (WS)
trim corners
① neaten edge
⅛ (0.3) ② single fold hem, then topstitch

gather frill to fit between armhole notches
* make two the same

2 sew front yoke

① stitch
FRONT YOKE FACING (WS)
② trim seam allowance to ¼ (0.5)
FRONT YOKE (RS)
③ turn yoke RS out
press seam towards facing
FRONT YOKE FACING (RS)
FRONT YOKE (WS)

3 sew back yoke

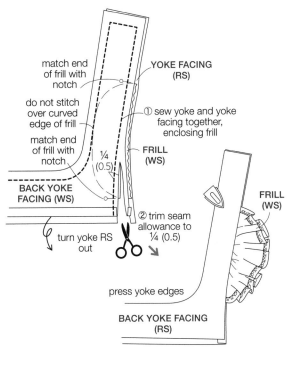

match end of frill with notch

do not stitch over curved edge of frill

match end of frill with notch

YOKE FACING (RS)

① sew yoke and yoke facing together, enclosing frill

FRILL (WS)

BACK YOKE FACING (WS)

¼ (0.5)

② trim seam allowance to ¼ (0.5)

turn yoke RS out

press yoke edges

FRILL (WS)

BACK YOKE FACING (RS)

4 sew side seams

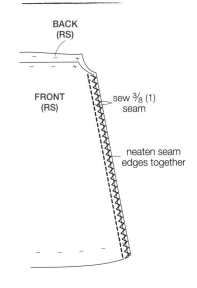

BACK (RS)

FRONT (RS)

sew ⅜ (1) seam

neaten seam edges together

5 sew facings to armholes

ARMHOLE FACING (WS)

① stitch ⅜ (1)

¼ (0.7)

② trim seam allowance to ¼ (0.5)

③ clip curves

BACK (RS)

side seam

FRONT (RS)

↓

ARMHOLE FACING (RS)

topstitch ¼ (0.7)

BACK (RS)

FRONT (WS)

¹⁄₁₆ (0.1)

side seam

6 sew yokes to dress

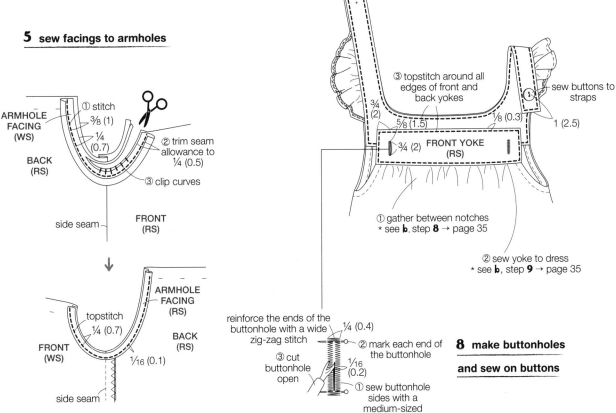

③ topstitch around all edges of front and back yokes

sew buttons to straps

¾ (2)

⅝ (1.5)

⅛ (0.3)

1 (2.5)

¾ (2)

FRONT YOKE (RS)

① gather between notches
* see **b**, step **8** → page 35

② sew yoke to dress
* see **b**, step **9** → page 35

reinforce the ends of the buttonhole with a wide zig-zag stitch

¼ (0.4)

② mark each end of the buttonhole

③ cut buttonhole open

¹⁄₁₆ (0.2)

① sew buttonhole sides with a medium-sized zig-zag stitch

8 make buttonholes and sew on buttons

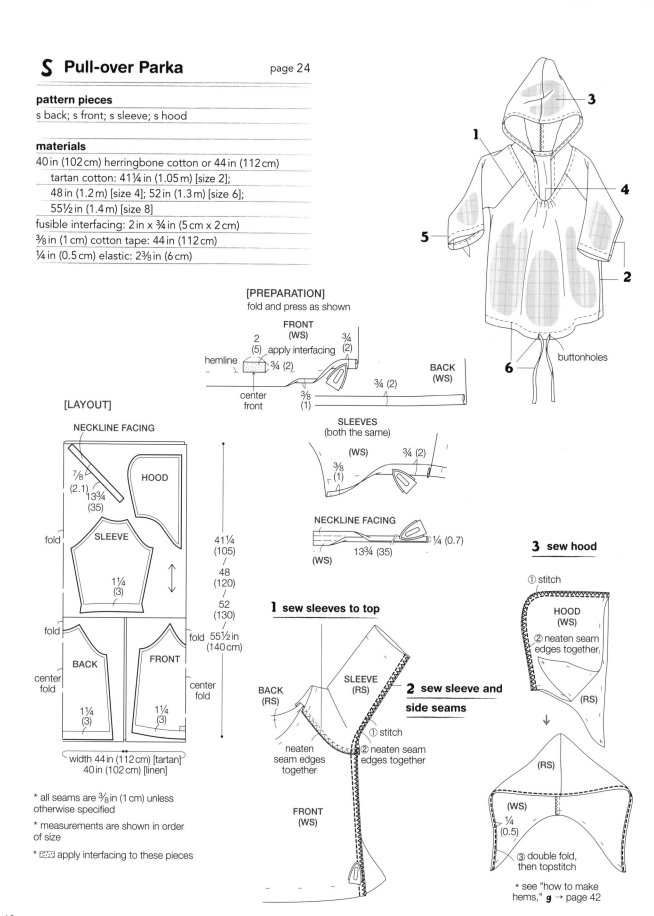

S Pull-over Parka

page 24

pattern pieces

s back; s front; s sleeve; s hood

materials

40 in (102 cm) herringbone cotton or 44 in (112 cm) tartan cotton: 41¼ in (1.05 m) [size 2]; 48 in (1.2 m) [size 4]; 52 in (1.3 m) [size 6]; 55½ in (1.4 m) [size 8]

fusible interfacing: 2 in x ¾ in (5 cm x 2 cm)

⅜ in (1 cm) cotton tape: 44 in (112 cm)

¼ in (0.5 cm) elastic: 2⅜ in (6 cm)

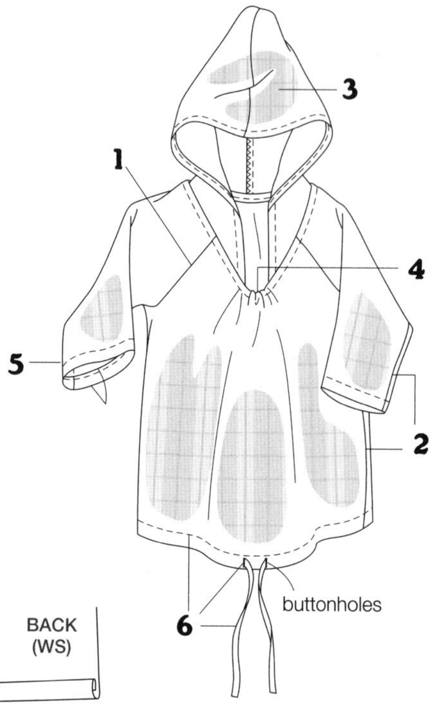

1
2
3
4
5
6
buttonholes

[PREPARATION]

fold and press as shown

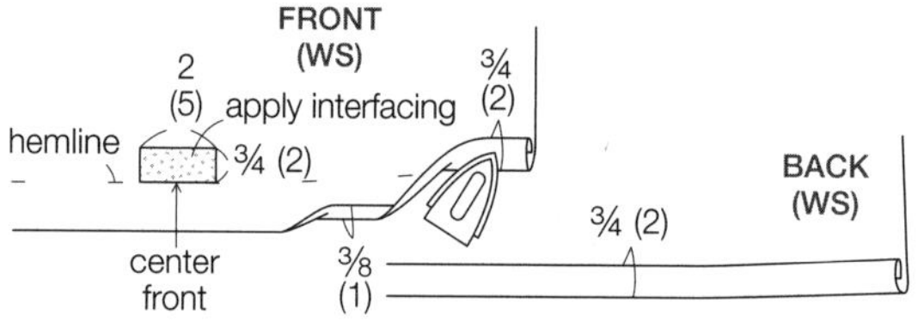

FRONT
(WS)
2
(5)
apply interfacing
hemline
¾ (2)
¾
(2)
center
front
⅜
(1)
¾ (2)
BACK
(WS)

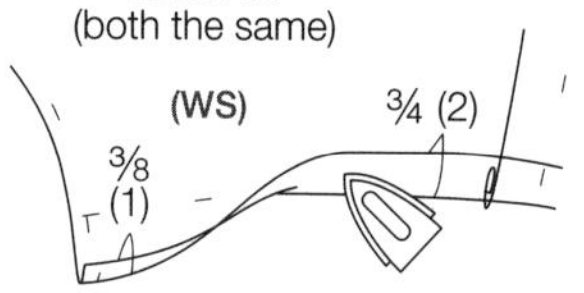

SLEEVES
(both the same)
(WS)
¾ (2)
⅜
(1)

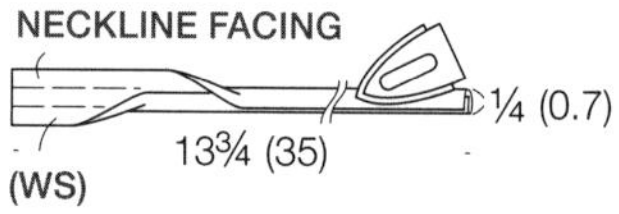

NECKLINE FACING
¼ (0.7)
13¾ (35)
(WS)

[LAYOUT]

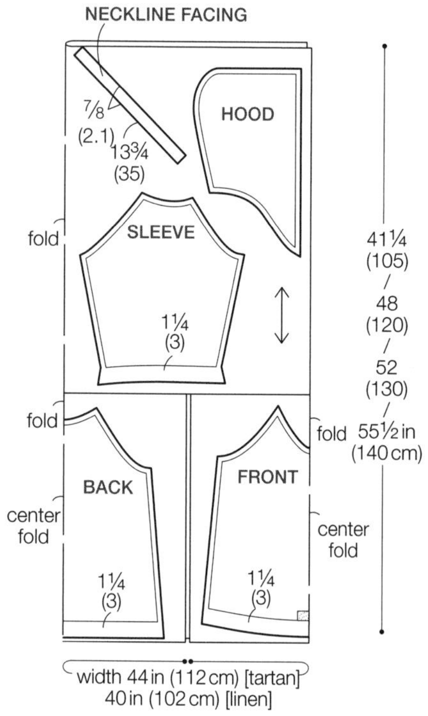

NECKLINE FACING
⅞
(2.1)
13¾
(35)
HOOD
fold
SLEEVE
1¼
(3)
41¼
(105)
/
48
(120)
/
52
(130)
/
55½ in
(140 cm)
fold
fold
BACK
FRONT
center
fold
center
fold
1¼
(3)
1¼
(3)
width 44 in (112 cm) [tartan]
40 in (102 cm) [linen]

* all seams are ⅜ in (1 cm) unless otherwise specified

* measurements are shown in order of size

* apply interfacing to these pieces

1 sew sleeves to top

2 sew sleeve and side seams

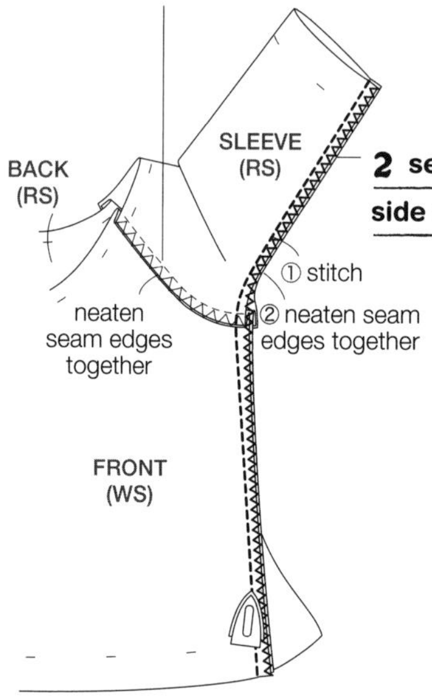

BACK
(RS)
SLEEVE
(RS)
① stitch
neaten
seam edges
together
② neaten seam
edges together
FRONT
(WS)

3 sew hood

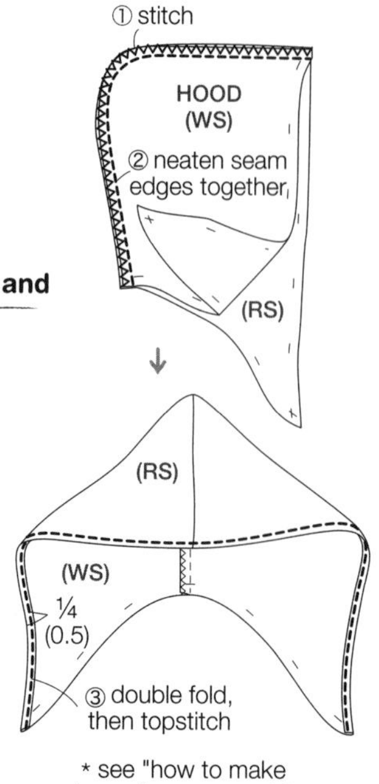

① stitch
HOOD
(WS)
② neaten seam
edges together
(RS)
(RS)
(WS)
¼
(0.5)
③ double fold,
then topstitch

* see "how to make hems," g → page 42

4 sew hood to top

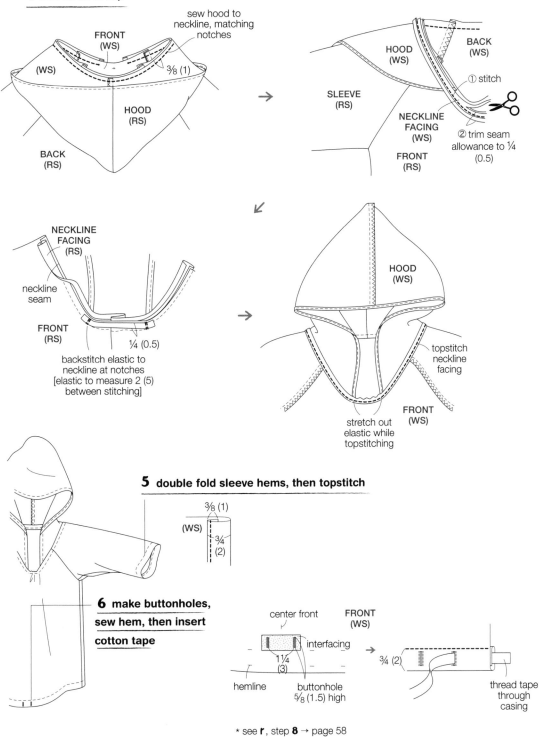

sew hood to neckline, matching notches

FRONT (WS)

(WS)

3/8 (1)

HOOD (RS)

BACK (RS)

HOOD (WS)

SLEEVE (RS)

BACK (WS)

① stitch

NECKLINE FACING (WS)

FRONT (RS)

② trim seam allowance to 1/4 (0.5)

NECKLINE FACING (RS)

neckline seam

FRONT (RS)

1/4 (0.5)

backstitch elastic to neckline at notches [elastic to measure 2 (5) between stitching]

HOOD (WS)

topstitch neckline facing

FRONT (WS)

stretch out elastic while topstitching

5 double fold sleeve hems, then topstitch

3/8 (1)

(WS)

3/4 (2)

6 make buttonholes, sew hem, then insert cotton tape

center front

FRONT (WS)

interfacing

1 1/4 (3)

hemline

buttonhole 5/8 (1.5) high

3/4 (2)

thread tape through casing

* see **r**, step **8** → page 58

✝ Boy's Shirt

page 25

pattern pieces

t back; t front; t sleeve; t yoke & yoke facing;
  t neck band; t collar

materials

48 in (120 cm) cotton: 41¼ in (1.05 m) [size 2];
  44 in (1.1 m) [size 4]; 45½ in (1.15 m) [size 6];
  48 in (1.2 m) [size 8]
fusible interfacing: 19¾ in x 19¾ in (50 cm x 50 cm)
⅜ in (1 cm) buttons x 6

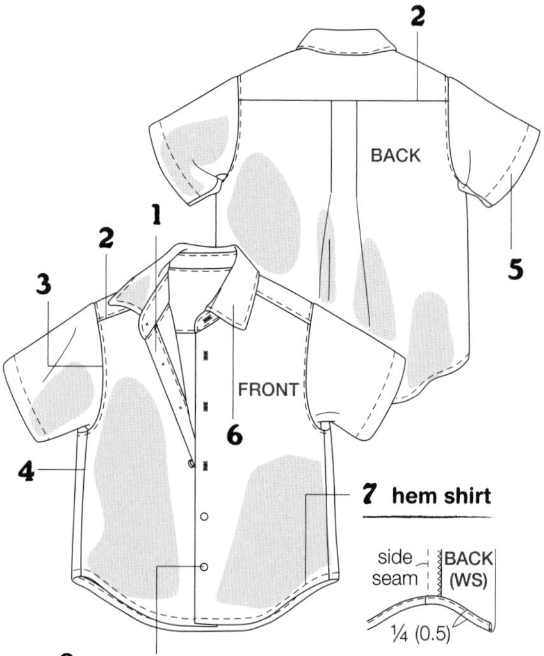

[LAYOUT]

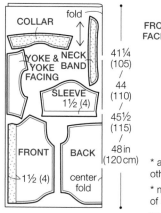

COLLAR
fold
YOKE & YOKE FACING
NECK BAND
SLEEVE 1½ (4)
FRONT 1½ (4)
BACK center fold

41¼ (105)
44 (110)
45½ (115)
48 in (120 cm)

← width 48 in (120 cm) →

FUSIBLE INTERFACING

FRONT FACING
COLLAR
NECK BAND

19¾ in (50 cm)
19¾ in (50 cm)

* all seams are ⅜ in (1 cm) unless otherwise specified

* measurements are shown in order of size

* ▨ apply interfacing to these pieces

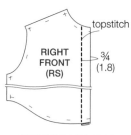

BACK
FRONT

7 hem shirt

side seam
BACK (WS)
¼ (0.5)

8 make buttonholes and sew on buttons

* see "how to make hems", **g** → page 42

---

2 sew yoke to shirt

③ fold and press shoulder edges of yoke facing

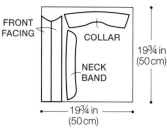

YOKE FACING (WS)
⅜ (1)
⅜ (1)
YOKE (WS)
① sew yoke and yoke facing together, enclosing top edge of shirt back
LEFT FRONT (RS)
⅜ (1)
RIGHT FRONT (RS)
② sew yoke to shirt front pieces
BACK (RS)

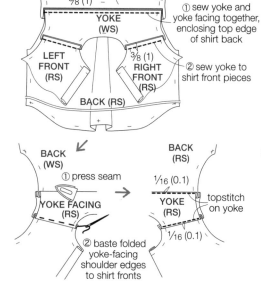

BACK (WS)
① press seam
YOKE FACING (RS)
② baste folded yoke-facing shoulder edges to shirt fronts

BACK (RS)
1/16 (0.1)
YOKE (RS)
topstitch on yoke
1/16 (0.1)

[PREPARATION]

fold and press as shown

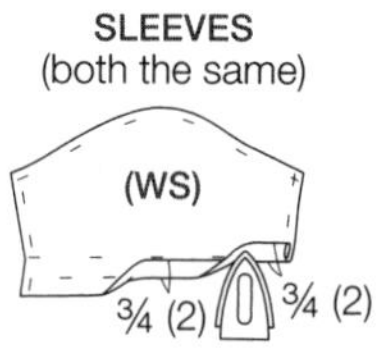

SLEEVES
(both the same)

(WS)
¾ (2)   ¾ (2)

apply interfacing to upper collar and upper neckband only

(WS) UPPER COLLAR
(WS) UPPER NECKBAND

apply interfacing to front plackets (left and right sides)

1½ (4)
use a press cloth when ironing on interfacing
(WS)
¾ (2)
¾ (2)

press back tuck

1¼ (3)
(RS)

1 sew front placket

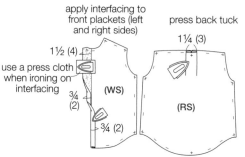

topstitch
RIGHT FRONT (RS)
¾ (1.8)

fold left front the same but do not topstitch

4 sew sleeve and side seams

3 sew sleeves to shirt

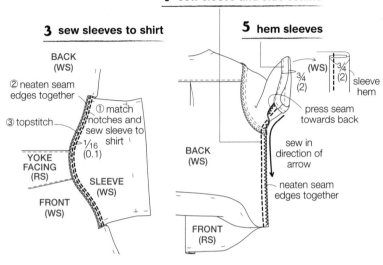

BACK (WS)

② neaten seam edges together

③ topstitch

① match notches and sew sleeve to shirt

$^{1}/_{16}$ (0.1)

YOKE FACING (RS)

SLEEVE (WS)

FRONT (WS)

5 hem sleeves

(WS) $^{3}/_{4}$ (2)

$^{3}/_{4}$ (2)

sleeve hem

press seam towards back

BACK (WS)

sew in direction of arrow

FRONT (RS)

neaten seam edges together

6 make collar

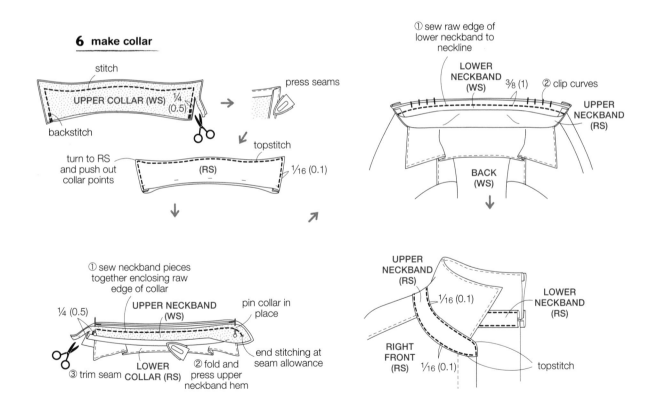

stitch

UPPER COLLAR (WS) $^{1}/_{4}$ (0.5)

backstitch

press seams

turn to RS and push out collar points

topstitch

(RS) $^{1}/_{16}$ (0.1)

① sew neckband pieces together enclosing raw edge of collar

$^{1}/_{4}$ (0.5)

UPPER NECKBAND (WS)

pin collar in place

LOWER COLLAR (RS)

③ trim seam

② fold and press upper neckband hem

end stitching at seam allowance

① sew raw edge of lower neckband to neckline

LOWER NECKBAND (WS)

$^{3}/_{8}$ (1)

② clip curves

UPPER NECKBAND (RS)

BACK (WS)

UPPER NECKBAND (RS)

$^{1}/_{16}$ (0.1)

LOWER NECKBAND (RS)

RIGHT FRONT (RS)

$^{1}/_{16}$ (0.1)

topstitch

63

Published in 2013 by Tuttle Publishing, an imprint of Periplus Editions (HK) Ltd.

www.tuttlepublishing.com

ISBN 978-4-8053-1286-5
Library of Congress Cataloging-in-Publication data for this book is in progress

Happy Homemade vol.2
Kids no fundangi
by Ruriko Yamada

Copyright © 2009 by EDUCATIONAL FOUNDATION BUNKA GAKUEN
BUNKA PUBLISHING BUREAU
Originally published in Japan in 2009 by EDUCATIONAL FOUNDATION
BUNKA GAKUEN BUNKA PUBLISHING BUREAU
World English translation rights arranged with EDUCATIONAL FOUNDATION
BUNKA GAKUEN BUNKA PUBLISHING BUREAU through THE ENGLISH
AGENCY (JAPAN) LTD.

* p26–32 excerpt from Sewing Recipe: Master Sewing Techniques as You
Go. Yoshiko Tsukiori Basic Technique. (Author: Yoshiko Tsukiori, Photography:
Yasuo Nagumo. Publisher: EDUCATIONAL FOUNDATION BUNKA GAKUEN
BUNKA PUBLISHING BUREAU)

First published in the English language by Penguin Group (Australia), 2012
English translation copyright © Penguin Group (Australia), 2012

The moral right of the author has been asserted

Publisher of the original Japanese edition: Sunao Onuma
Cover and text design by Hiroko Nakajima
Photography by Mie Morimoto
Sewing instruction and digital tracing by Shikano Room
Real-size pattern grading by Kazuhiro Ueno
Styling by Kiyomi Shiraogawa
Hair and make-up by Yumi Narai
Modelling by Francis Tamamo, Korari Kawamata, Hibiki Yano

English language edition
Cover and text design by Claire Tice and Marley Flory (Penguin ed)
English adaptation series editor: Felicity Dawson
Translation by Masashi Karasawa
Pattern adaptation by Felicity Dawson
Pattern tracing by Nikki Townsend

Distributed by

North America, Latin America & Europe
Tuttle Publishing
364 Innovation Drive, North Clarendon, VT 05759-9436 U.S.A.
Tel: 1 (802) 773-8930; Fax: 1 (802) 773-6993
info@tuttlepublishing.com; www.tuttlepublishing.com

Japan
Tuttle Publishing
Yaekari Building, 3rd Floor, 5-4-12 Osaki, Shinagawa-ku, Tokyo 141 0032
Tel: (81) 3 5437-0171; Fax: (81) 3 5437-0755
sales@tuttle.co.jp; www.tuttle.co.jp

Asia Pacific
Berkeley Books Pte. Ltd.
61 Tai Seng Avenue #02-12, Singapore 534167
Tel: (65) 6280-1330; Fax: (65) 6280-6290
inquiries@periplus.com.sg; www.periplus.com

Printed in China   1307RP
16 15 14 13   6 5 4 3 2 1

TUTTLE PUBLISHING® is a registered trademark of Tuttle Publishing,
a division of Periplus Editions (HK) Ltd.

The Tuttle Story
"Books to Span the East and West"

Most people are surprised to learn that the world's largest publisher of books on Asia had its humble beginnings in the tiny American state of Vermont. The company's founder, Charles Tuttle, came from a New England family steeped in publishing, and his first love was books—especially old and rare editions.

Tuttle's father was a noted antiquarian dealer in Rutland, Vermont. Young Charles honed his knowledge of the trade working in the family bookstore, and later in the rare books section of Columbia University Library. His passion for beautiful books—old and new—never wavered throughout his long career as a bookseller and publisher.

After graduating from Harvard, Tuttle enlisted in the military and in 1945 was sent to Tokyo to work on General Douglas MacArthur's staff. He was tasked with helping to revive the Japanese publishing industry, which had been utterly devastated by the war. When his tour of duty was completed, he left the military, married a talented and beautiful singer, Reiko Chiba, and in 1948 began several successful business ventures.

To his astonishment, Tuttle discovered that postwar Tokyo was actually a book-lover's paradise. He befriended dealers in the Kanda district and began supplying rare Japanese editions to American libraries. He also imported American books to sell to the thousands of GIs stationed in Japan. By 1949, Tuttle's business was thriving, and he opened Tokyo's very first English-language bookstore in the Takashimaya Department Store in Ginza, to great success. Two years later, he began publishing books to fulfill the growing interest of foreigners in all things Asian.

Though a westerner, Tuttle was hugely instrumental in bringing a knowledge of Japan and Asia to a world hungry for information about the East. By the time of his death in 1993, he had published over 6,000 books on Asian culture, history and art—a legacy honored by Emperor Hirohito in 1983 with the "Order of the Sacred Treasure," the highest honor Japan bestows upon non-Japanese.

The Tuttle company today maintains an active backlist of some 1,500 titles, many of which have been continuously in print since the 1950s and 1960s—a great testament to Charles Tuttle's skill as a publisher. More than 60 years after its founding, Tuttle Publishing is more active today than at any time in its history, still inspired by Charles Tuttle's core mission—to publish fine books to span the East and West and provide a greater understanding of each.